Belair Early Years

Waterplay

Jean Evans

Acknowledgements

The author and publishers would like to thank the staff and children of Early Steps Nursery, Ferndene Nursery, Kids and Co Nursery, Osmotherley Pre-school, Selby Cottage Childcare Centre and Whinney Banks Nursery for their invaluable help in the production of this book.

The author would like to say a special 'thank you' to Brenda Curry, Elizabeth Wigington and Sue Welburn for their additional help. She would also like to thank her daughters, Sally and Charlotte, for their assistance in setting up some of the activities.

Noah and the Ark (page 60)

First published in 2000 by BELAIR PUBLICATIONS LIMITED
Albert House, Apex Business Centre, Boscombe Road, Dunstable, Beds, LU5 4RL

Reprinted 2004.

Editor: Elizabeth Miles Design: Jane Conway Page layout: Philippa Jarvis Photography: Kelvin Freeman and Penny Shepherd
Cover design: Ed Gallagher

ISBN 0 94788 252 9

Contents

Introduction

The aim of this series is to provide resource material covering all the main areas of young children's learning. Each book is a 64-page full colour resource, designed specifically for educators, which provides practical 'hands on' activities suitable for working with the under-fives. They also provide a variety of starting points to encourage and promote creative play.

Written by professionals working in early years education, each book is organised into popular themes providing ideas to develop the linguistic, mathematical, scientific, creative, environmental, and personal and social areas of learning. The key learning intentions are provided for each theme.

Full colour photography offers ideas and inspiration for presenting and developing children's individual work with creative ideas for display. An additional feature of each book is the 'Home Links' section. This provides extension ideas and activities for children to develop at home for each theme. One other particular focus of *Waterplay* is that of the importance of preparation of the learning environment to make the most effective use of waterplay activities.

The aim of this book is to demonstrate how a simple water tray can be transformed into a stimulating focus point for a wide range of learning activities. A brief explanation of how to set up the water tray for each particular theme is included, together with any additional resources needed. The themes can be used on their own as stimuli for waterplay, or can be included in the planning of a nursery theme or related subject.

- **The Environment**
  The first four themes are linked to the environment. Children will learn more about the world around them as they explore life under the sea and in ponds, discover features of the North and South polar regions, and make their own water garden.

- **Science**
  These activities introduce children to a range of science topics as they experiment with ideas, such as floating and sinking, and discover how things move across water.

- **The Senses**
  Young children are very aware of sensory experiences. The two sensory themes encourage them to respond to things they smell, taste, see and touch as they learn about colours and make vegetable mixtures.

- **Caring for Ourselves**
  The caring themes introduce children to the need for personal hygiene and clean clothes as they explore their daily routines. Comparisons are made between how clothes are washed today and how they were washed in the past.

- **Rhymes and Stories**
  The acquisition of language and a love of literacy are important parts of children's development. The children will have great fun with the activities that focus on water-related rhymes as they pretend to make tea and create rain effects. Two story themes, one from the ancient story of a great flood and another from a well-known series of children's books, are used as stimuli for work on the weather and on plumbing.

Water Tray Area

A well-planned area where children have easy access to a variety of different resources can extend considerably the learning opportunities offered by waterplay.

Water Trays

- A round tray enables several children to have equal access to the contents and encourages co-operation.
- Transparent trays are a good choice as they allow children to see what is happening to objects in the water and to observe changes of colour.
- Trays with moulded shapes and built-in working parts, such as wheels and lock-gates, provide additional challenges and stimulate curiosity as to how things work.
- A baby's bath or a large bowl are satisfactory alternatives to water trays.

Additional Resources

- Do not put too many resources out at any one time. Children need to be able to make choices easily and to see the results of their actions on the water.
- Items such as sets of graded containers and funnels will extend the range of learning opportunities. Alternatively, use recycled items of different sizes, such as plastic bottles, cartons and tubes.
- Fill small baskets with collections of different resources, such as small stones, sponge pieces, corks, twigs, shells, small model figures and sea creatures. Change the contents frequently.
- Ensure that some resources float and others sink. Pierce holes in plastic containers at different levels for experimentation.
- Fit a plank across the water tray, using wooden wedges to stop it slipping. This will provide a useful platform on which the children can stand the containers they are filling. Alternatively, position a table at the end of the water tray and cover it with a towel.
- Drill holes of different diameters in the plank so that children can fit funnels and pipes into the holes to pour water through.

Storage of Resources

- A wide variety of wire storage racks can be obtained from educational suppliers' catalogues, or use a simple vegetable rack.
- Display smaller resources, such as corks and plastic animals, in seed trays, on a shelf or on a table.
- Ideally, children should be able to see all the equipment easily so that they can make choices and return items to a designated place when they have finished with them. Make sticky-backed plastic silhouettes of each item and attach them to a screen, shelf or table top.
- Tie string to the handles of equipment, such as spoons and whisks, and hang these on plastic hooks attached to screens.

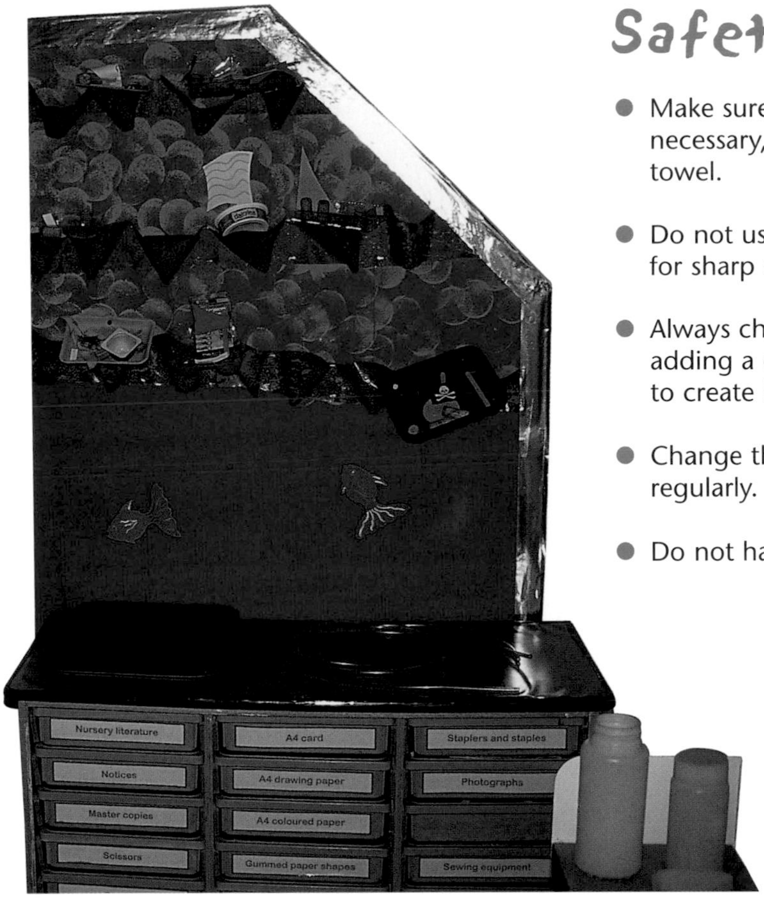

Safety

- Make sure the floor is non-slip and protect it, if necessary, with a safety mat, newspapers or a large towel.
- Do not use any glass containers and check all items for sharp edges.
- Always check for allergies to substances before adding a colour or a perfume to the water, or a soap to create bubbles.
- Change the water daily and wash all resources regularly.
- Do not handle ice straight from the freezer.

Comfort

- Make sure the children roll up their sleeves before beginning an activity.
- Always have spare dry clothes available.
- Do not have the water too cold or let the children handle ice for too long.
- Limit the number of children playing at the water tray at any one time to avoid overcrowding.

Displays

- Hang a sign in the area, inviting children to 'Come and play with the water'. Indicate the number allowed in the area at any one time.
- Create charts for parents or carers to read about the learning opportunities offered through waterplay. Suspend these as mobiles or attach them to a wall or a screen.
- Make the area attractive by cutting a piece of thick card into the shape of large drops of water. Write appropriate words on some of the drops, such as 'splash', 'trickle' and 'drip', and cover the other drops with silver and blue foil. Attach them all to threads and hang from the ceiling.

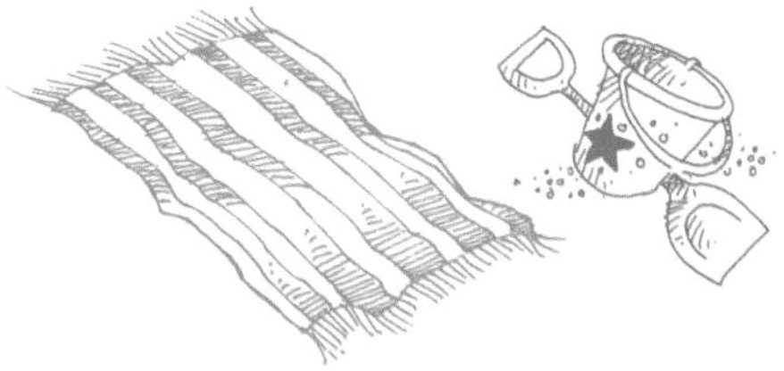

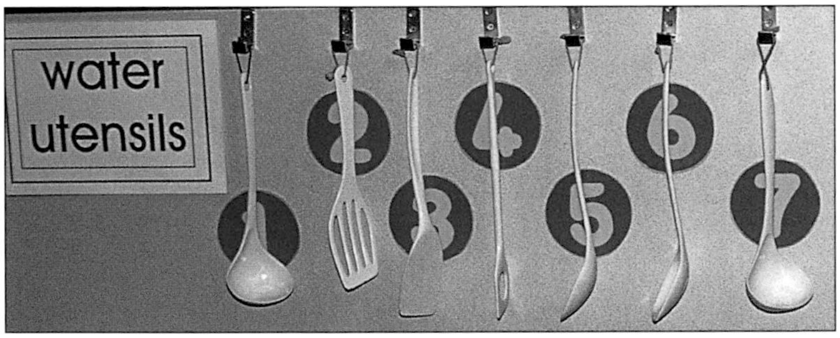

Accessories

- Check that there are enough accessible trays and boxes so that the children can keep the area tidy themselves.
- Provide an absorbent mop and a bucket for cleaning up spills.
- Ensure that aprons are easy to put on. Hang them on plastic hooks at a suitable height.
- Hang up a towel next to the aprons.

Under the Sea

Learning Intentions

- To explore the features of living things and natural materials.
- To count, sort and match everyday objects.

Starting Point

- Look at books about the sea and pictures of under the sea. Talk about creatures that live in the sea. Discuss what the bottom of the sea looks like and whether any plants grow there.

Setting Up

- Prepare the water tray by spreading a thin layer of sand across the bottom and adding a selection of small rocks, shells and stones.

- Decorate the edges of the tray with blue and green crêpe paper strips to give the effect of flowing water.
- Fill the tray slowly with water and experiment by adding blue and green food colouring to make a sea-water colour. Allow the sand to settle.
- Make seaweed with strands of green Cellophane and anchor them by tucking the ends under the stones.
- Prepare a resource table with a selection of sea creatures, toy boats and seaside buckets.

Language and Literacy

- Draw around each object on sticky-backed plastic and cut out the shapes to make silhouettes. Stick these to a washable surface at well-spaced intervals. Arrange the objects on the silhouettes.
- Create a rock pool area for role-play using an inflated paddling pool. Position the pool near the water tray and arrange pebbles and shells on the bottom before adding water. Drape green Cellophane over the edge to represent seaweed.
- Place a large yellow sheet around the edge of the pool to represent sand and arrange rocks, pebbles and shells on it. Add children's towels, beach toys and fishing nets. Create a 'wind-break' from a clothes-horse draped in brightly coloured fabric.

- Develop imaginative play in the water tray and rock pool area by encouraging the children to make up their own 'under the sea' stories. For example, build an underwater cave from stones for a mystery creature, or uncover a valuable treasure buried in the rock pool.
- Extend the children's vocabulary as you introduce life under the sea, such as fish, jellyfish, eels, sea horses and seaweed. Write labels for these to add to a wall frieze.
- Find items beginning with 's' on the display, such as sea, sand and seaweed. Repeat with other letters.
- Encourage the children to talk about holidays or trips to the coast. Talk about their experiences of the sea. Did they paddle or swim in the sea?

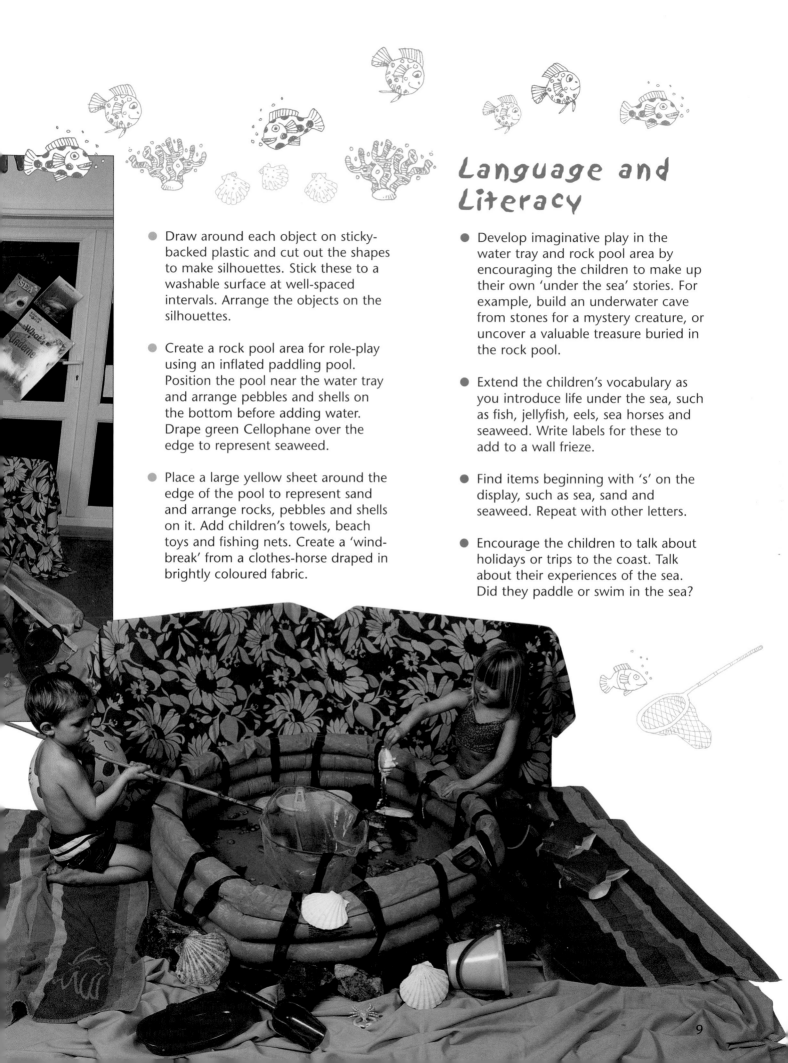

Mathematics

- Use mathematical language to describe the positions of items in the water tray. What is on the bottom of the sea? What do fish swim above? Which items float on the top?
- Match the sea creatures to their silhouettes. See how many the children can name. Ask questions such as: 'What is next to the crab?' 'How many legs has the starfish?'
- Sort a selection of plastic animals and fish into two piles according to whether they live on land or under the sea.

- Play a fishing game. Cut fish shapes from thick plastic and number them from 1 to 5 on both sides using waterproof pens. Attach two paper-clips to the mouth of each fish and put them in the pool. Make fishing rods from canes with string attached and tie a magnet to the end of each string. Each child chooses a seaside bucket and fishing rod and tries to catch a set of fish numbered from 1 to 5 from the paddling pool. Ask appropriate questions such as: 'How many more do we need?' Use words such as 'most', 'least' and 'same'.
- Learn the number rhyme 'One, two, three, four, five, Once I caught a fish alive ...'.

Our World

- Take the paper-clips off some of the fish in the pool, mix them all up and try catching them again. Sort them into two piles according to whether or not they can be picked up with a fishing rod magnet.
- Look at pictures in books and at plastic models to find similarities and differences between creatures that live in the sea and those that live on land.
- Scoop up some of the sand and water from the water tray in a transparent plastic container. Ask the children to suggest how they could separate the two. Put some filter paper in a funnel and pour the mixture through it. What do the children notice? Had they guessed correctly?

Creative Work

- Create an 'under the sea' wall frieze. Begin by looking at books and pictures and talking about items the children would like to include. Use a range of painting techniques, such as combing thick paint to create a wave effect and sponging white paint on the surface of the sea to represent foam. Add different textures, such as pieces of fishing net, sponge and cork.

- Paint sea animals or use collage materials. Introduce stimulating textures as you make fish, crabs and boats to add to the scene.

- Create sand pictures by painting swirls with glue and sprinkling sand on top.

- Make 'shell' pendants from salt dough or clay. Pierce a hole in the shell-shape before baking, to attach a ribbon.

Home Links

- Send home silhouettes of land and sea creatures for children and parents to cut out and stick to a sheet of paper to make a picture.

Ask parents or carers to:

- discuss the creatures on the sheet as they work with the children and encourage them to find similar creatures in books

- help their children to make a book about an outing to the seaside, a boat trip or a visit to a sea-life centre. Include items such as photographs, artefacts and brochures.

Pond Fishing

Learning Intentions

- To look for similarities, differences and changes in living things by exploring their features.
- To count and recognise the numerals 1 to 5 and to begin to use the vocabulary involved in addition and subtraction.

Starting Points

- Look at books and pictures about ponds and talk about the creatures that live there.
- Talk about what the bottom of a pond looks like and the kinds of plants that grow in a pond.
- You might visit a pond and fish with nets (you may need to get permission from the relevant authority). Explore your catch with magnifying glasses and make observational drawings before returning it to the pond.

Setting Up

- Place a layer of pebbles on the bottom of a transparent water tray and fill the tray with water coloured with food colouring. Add green Cellophane to represent weeds and bubble wrap for frog spawn.
- Use coloured plastic materials, such as refuse sacks, carrier bags and off-cuts of vinyl floor covering, to make creatures such as fish, frogs and tadpoles for the pond tray.
- Add plastic models of frogs, tadpoles, fish and insects, such as dragonflies, to the pond. Include a log and some large stones for the creatures to sit on.
- Cover a table in green fabric and display a frog container (see Language and Literacy), books about frogs and tadpoles, and any other appropriate resources.
- On a table near the pond tray, arrange a selection of items to fish with, such as soup ladles, sieves, small fishing nets and some small buckets.

Mathematics

- Play a fishing game in groups. Each child chooses a bucket and something to fish with, such as a spoon, a sieve or a cup, and goes fishing. Use a timer to see how many things can be caught in one minute. Tip out the contents into the buckets and talk about the catch.

- Count the number of creatures caught in one minute.

- Sit five plastic frogs on a branch in the table-top pond (see Creative Work). Write the numbers 1 to 5 on squares of card and arrange next to the frogs. Sing the number rhyme 'Five Speckled Frogs'. At the end of each verse, a child makes a frog jump into the pool and another child removes the relevant number card. Use phrases such as 'one more', 'take one away' and 'how many are left?' as you play.

Language and Literacy

- Make a frog container to house children's name cards. Roll back the edges of a strong paper sack, paint the outside green, and the inside pink for the mouth. Glue on scrunched up paper eyes (with black-paper pupils). Ask the children to put their name card in the frog's mouth when they visit the display.

- Sing the rhyme 'Five little Speckled Frogs' by Jan Betts from *Knock At the Door*. Emphasise the rhyming words ('frog', 'log'; 'pool', 'cool'). Can they think of other words that rhyme with 'log', such as 'fog', 'dog', 'bog'?

- Look at books on pond life. Introduce appropriate vocabulary, such as 'illustration', 'page', 'word', 'letter' and 'author'.

Our World

- Discuss the life cycle of a frog. Handle models of the different stages and make a zigzag 'feely' book using bubble wrap for frog spawn, scraps of refuse sacks for tadpoles, and green and brown felt for frogs. Arrange as a table display.

- If possible, arrange a display on a nearby table with a small fish tank so that the children can observe goldfish. Include appropriate books, writing tools and other materials for the children to make observational drawings.

- Talk about how fish breathe and move. Introduce the words 'gills' and 'fins'. Ask: 'What do fish eat?' Make comparisons with how the children breathe and move, and what they like to eat.

- Put a sample of pond water into a small tank for the children to observe with magnifying glasses. Try to ensure that there are some live creatures in the sample, or buy some pond snails from a garden centre or pet shop. Return the sample to the pond after a couple of days.

- Look at books and discover the names of other pond creatures, such as water boatmen and dragonflies. Compare pictures of the creatures, looking for similarities and differences.

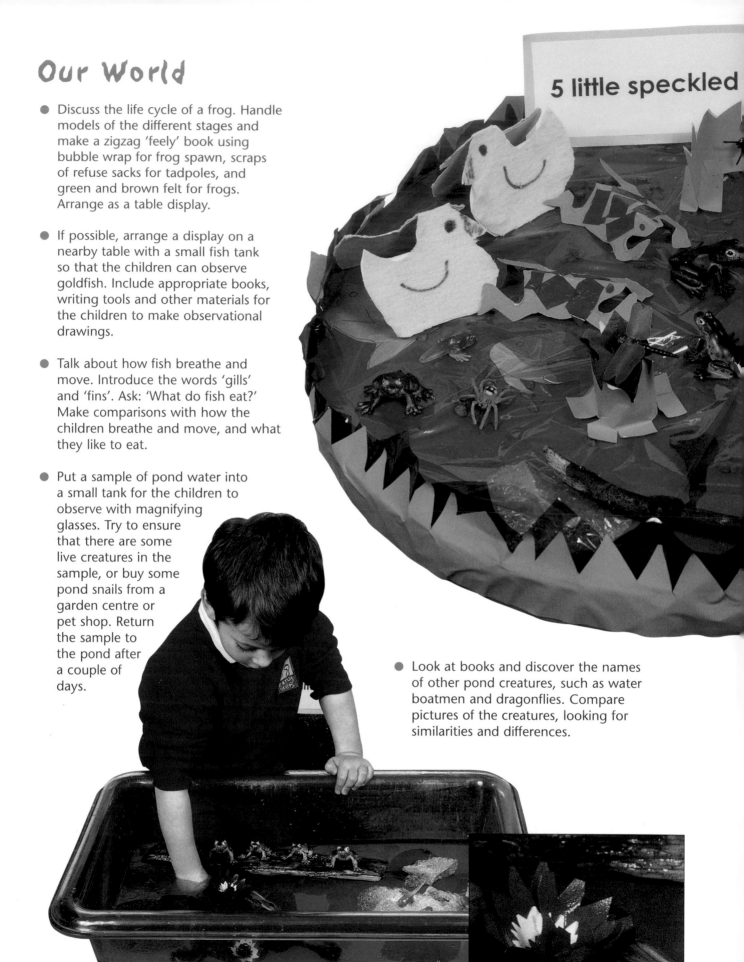

Creative Work

- Make some water lilies to float on the water tray. Use green Cellophane for the leaves and pink and white sugar paper for the flowers. Create the flower petals by cutting out star shapes from the sugar paper and sticking a white star on top of a pink star. Stick each flower to the centre of a leaf.
- Create pond pictures by mixing blobs of thick blue, green and white paint on a piece of paper, using fingers or a cardboard comb. Spread the paint out to form a pond shape. Add tissue strips for weed and pond creatures made from scraps of fabric.
- Make goldfish bowl pictures. Cut out a bowl shape from white card and mount on blue card cut to the same shape, but larger, to create a blue border. Use tissue and wallpaper pieces to make goldfish and pond weeds.
- Back a display board near the water tray with dark blue paper in the shape of a large pond and arrange the pictures, mounted on yellow paper or green paper, within the pond. Attach fishing nets to the sides of the display and entitle it 'Let's go fishing'.
- Create a pond on a small round table. Cover it with dark blue paper and arrange stones and fish made from coloured card on top. Spread blue Cellophane on top and secure with tape under the table. Tape scrunched-up green Cellophane around the outside and green card cut to represent grass. Using card and felt, make yellow ducks and green frogs to add to the pond.

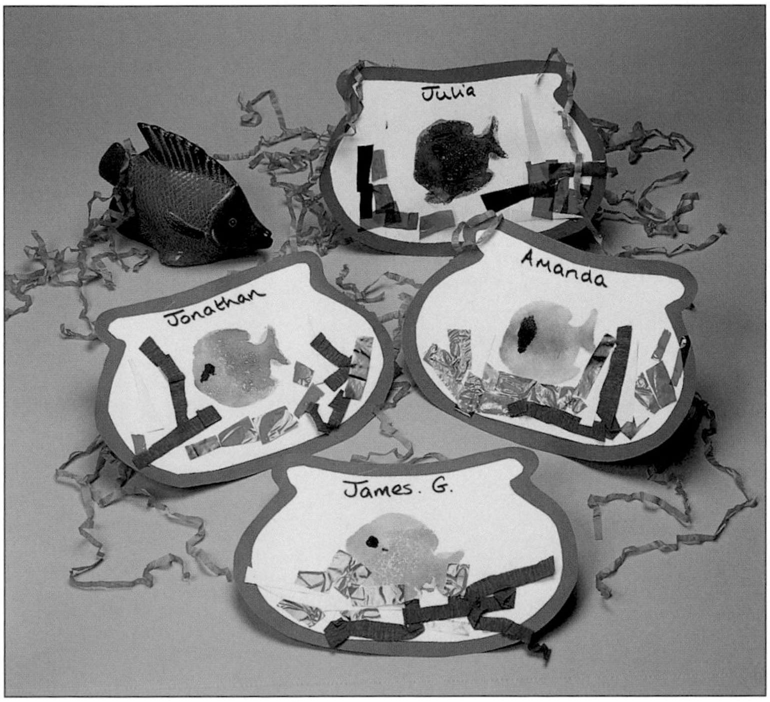

Home Links

Ask parents or carers to:

- take their children to a pond to observe pond life
- bring in samples of pond plants or creatures for display
- sing the number rhyme 'Five Little Speckled Frogs' with their children at bath-time, or using five model frogs.

North and South Poles

Learning Intentions

- To find out about the colder regions of the world and the creatures that live there.
- To investigate ice and discover some of its features.

Starting Points

- Look at books about and pictures of the creatures that live in the Arctic and Antarctic.
- Read appropriate stories, such as the 'Pingu' series.
- Look at a globe and point out the North and South Poles, and where the children live in relation to those places.
- Ask the children about their experiences of ice. Have they ever made ice cubes in the freezer? When do they eat ice lollies?
- Talk about Inuit life. What do Inuit people wear? Where do Inuits live? Discuss what it would be like to live in an igloo.

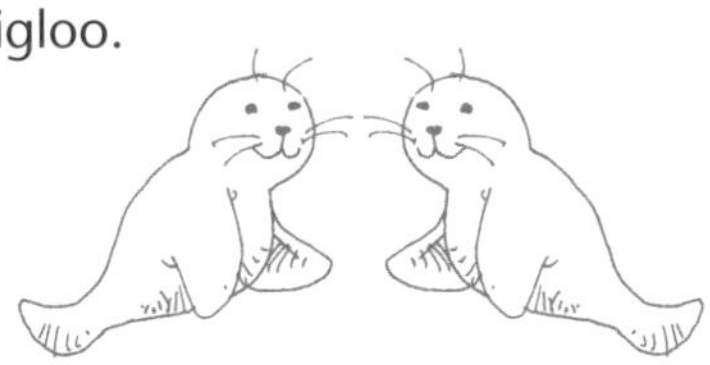

Setting Up

- The day before the planned activity, make ice in various containers, such as bowls, ice-cube holders and small sandwich boxes.
- Half-fill a transparent water tray with water and gradually add blue food colouring with a dropper. Watch as the drops hit the water. Let the children stir the water until it is a uniform colour.
- Add model creatures for an Arctic or an Antarctic scene (penguins live in the Antarctic and polar bears in the Arctic).
- Tip the prepared ice from the moulds into the water tray.

⚠ **Note:** Ice straight from the freezer burns fingers, so place the ice pieces in the water tray well before the children begin to handle it.

Our World

- Freeze a small bowl of water and tip the ice onto a piece of paper. Draw round the base, then place it in the water tray. Lift it out at regular intervals to draw round the base on the same piece of paper. What happens to the size of the circle? What is the reason for the changes?
- Add ice cubes to jugs of warm and cold water, then stir them round. Which ones melt first? Put some ice cubes outside in the sun, some in the refrigerator and some in a bowl on a radiator. Observe how quickly they melt.
- Discuss how we keep warm in cold weather. Find out what materials Inuit clothes are made of. What do the children wear to keep themselves warm?
- Fill identical plastic bottles with hand-hot water and wrap them in different materials, such as a woollen scarf, a cotton pillowcase, a polythene bag, a sheet of foil and a newspaper. Test the temperatures at regular intervals. Which stays warmest?

- Go outside on an icy day and look for frozen puddles. Is the ice slippery? Why is ice on the roads dangerous? Why is it dangerous to slide on frozen ponds? Sprinkle salt onto the puddles. What happens?
- Look at some ice skates and talk about ice rinks. Why do the skates have blades?
- Make some ice lollies in different colours, shapes and flavours. Which ones do the children like best?

Language and Literacy

- Encourage the children to play with the display and make up their own stories.
- Drop some ice blocks into the water tray. Describe how the water and the ice feel.
- Create a large igloo for role-play from a dome-shaped tent. Cover the tent in a white sheet marked with ice-block shapes. Encourage the children to talk about the features of a 'cold world' as they role-play.

Mathematics

- Create a number display with seals. Cut out seal shapes, pad with newspaper and add collage materials for texture. Add numbers for number recognition and counting.

- Put four quoits on a white towel to represent four holes in the snow. Using four model seals, ask the children questions such as: 'Is there a hole for each seal?' Add two more seals and ask: 'How many more holes are needed?'

Creative Work

- Make paper snowflakes by folding a circular piece of white paper three times and cutting shapes out of the folded edge. Open it out to reveal the snowflake.

- Prepare an interactive display about cold lands, or an Arctic or Antarctic display. Create a foil or blue paper backing. Glue collage penguins, seals, polar bears and whales to the backing. On a table, spread white wadding over a white sheet for snow and add circular pieces of blue foil for frozen pools. Place cardboard or toy models on the 'snow'. Label as appropriate.

- Cut penguin, igloo and Inuit shapes out of paper. Paint the penguins with a mixture of flour, water and paint for texture. Use white textured wallpaper, kitchen paper and cotton wool for the igloo. Outline each block of ice in black. Paint some wadding and then glue it to the Inuit to represent animal-skin clothing. Paint on additional features and display.

- For a 3D 'cold world' display, upturn bowls and cover with cotton wool for igloos. Paint cardboard tubes with black paint and attach to the back of decorated cardboard cut-out penguins so that they will stand up. Make Inuit figures from cardboard tubes. Glue on scraps of leather or brown fabric.

- Make icicles from blue or silver foil or white paper and hang them around the edge of wall displays and windows.

Home Links

Ask parents or carers to:

- let their children bring photographs of family or friends in the snow for display
- allow their children to bring in winter clothes on a named day
- help their children make ice lollies in various containers at home.

Water Garden

Learning Intentions

- To listen to and enjoy rhymes and stories.
- To make up stories during imaginative play.
- To investigate living things and to ask questions about why things happen.
- To use a wide range of tools.

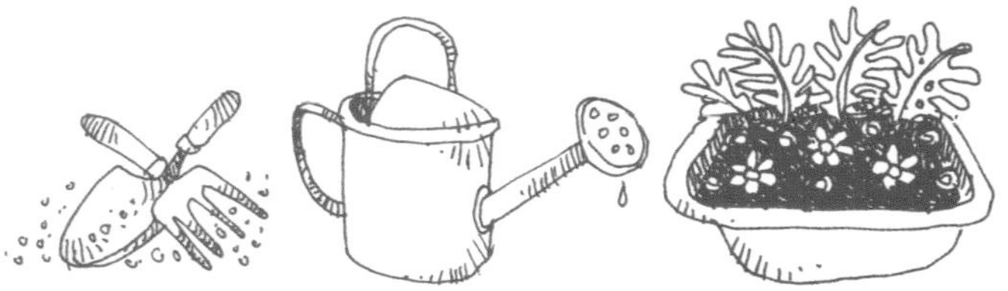

Starting Points

- Ask the children to bring in photographs or pictures of gardens. Discuss the different designs and colours.
- Collect leaflets from garden centres and send away for bulb catalogues.

Setting Up

- Create a stimulus table with plants, vases of flowers, small gardening tools and a watering can.
- Design a small-scale garden for miniature model people to enjoy. Draw a plan and plot the main items, such as a pond, lawn, bushes and vegetable plants.
- Create the garden by covering the bottom of a shallow water tray, baby's bath or builder's mixing tray with pebbles for drainage, followed by a layer of sand and a layer of compost.
- Press a bowl into the compost to form a depression for a pond. Line with black plastic and put gravel in the bottom and small pebbles around the sides. Fill with water and arrange small model frogs and ducks around and in the pond.

- Mark out paths around the garden to separate different areas. Create a seating area using flat stones and lengths of branch for seats.
- Make tiny buildings, such as a shed or greenhouse, from recycled boxes, and add play equipment for the model people, such as a miniature slide or swing.
- Plant grass seeds to create a lawn and experiment with small spider plants, herbs, moss and carrot tops for bushes. Plant cress and well-soaked beans and peas in the vegetable plot.
- Cover the tray with clingfilm to speed up seed germination. Water the garden daily with a toy watering can and cut the grass with scissors.
- Paint pictures of flowers, cut them out and mount them on backing paper to form a wall display.
- Create a 'Five Little Ducks' interactive display on a nearby table. Cover the table with artificial grass and make a pond from blue foil, paper or fabric. Arrange stones and leaves around the edge of the pond. Put a large plastic mother duck on the pond and five smaller ducks on the table. Make some number cards from 1 to 5 and arrange these on the table.

Language and Literacy

- Read the poems in the section 'In the garden and in the country' in *This Little Puffin*, edited by Elizabeth Matterson.
- Read and sing 'Five Little Ducks' by Ian Beck.
- Read stories such as the *Percy the Park-keeper* series by Nick Butterworth and *Meg's Veg* by Helen Nicholl. Talk about the things that are grown in the gardens in the stories.
- Make a book of the children's plans for their garden ideas. Ask them to describe their plans and write what they say in the book.
- Encourage the children to make up their own stories and act them out with the miniature people in their garden.

Mathematics

- Use the ducks on the table to act out the rhyme 'Five Little Ducks'. Start with the mother duck on the pond and arrange the small ducks in a line on the grass, swimming 'far away'. Put a number card beside each small duck. Take away a duck and a card as each one fails to return to the pond. Talk about how many are left each time.
- Use finger puppets (see Creative Work) to sing the rhyme 'Five Little Ducks'. Put the mother duck on one hand and the small ducks on the other. As one duck 'stays behind' remove a puppet from a finger and count how many remain.

Our World

- Visit a garden centre to buy seeds or small plants for your garden.
- Try to visit an allotment and ask a gardener to talk about what is growing there.

- Talk about the things seeds need to germinate, and the conditions needed for growth. Experimenting with cress seeds is an easy way to investigate this. Leave some without water, some in a dark room and some in good light. Try different growing mediums, such as soil, compost, cotton wool and absorbent tissues. Which is the most effective?
- Develop a small plot outdoors or use a water tray to create a miniature garden. Encourage the children to care for the plants, weeding and watering regularly.
- Experiment with a range of tiny tools, such as tweezers and salt spoons, to pick up seeds and transfer soil.

Creative Work

- Use collage materials to create textured garden pictures. For example, make brightly coloured flowers from fabric scraps and Cellophane, grass from green wool or raffia, leaves from green plastic and blossom from scrunched-up tissue paper.
- Cut out pictures of flowers from catalogues and use them to make pictures of flower gardens.
- Make one large mother duck finger puppet and five baby duck finger puppets and sing the rhyme 'Five Little Ducks' (see Mathematics). Make the puppets using a template, cutting felt to the correct shape. Draw round the template twice for each duck and stick the two pieces of felt together around the edge, leaving the bottom open for a finger or thumb. Add an orange felt beak and sequin eyes.

Home Links

Ask parents or carers to:

- encourage their children to sing the rhyme 'Five Little Ducks' (supply the words if necessary)
- accompany their children on a visit to a garden centre
- allow the children to visit their garden or allotment.

Floating and Sinking

Learning Intentions

- To investigate displacement, and floating and sinking.
- To record observations and to question why things happen.
- To use language associated with size, shape, position and quantity.
- To sort, count, match and make comparisons between objects that float and objects that sink.

Starting Points

- Read *Mr Archimedes' Bath* by Pamela Allen as an introduction to the concept of displacement. What happens when the animals get in the bath with Mr Archimedes? Does the water level rise or sink? Do the children think there is more or less water in the bath?
- Discuss things that the children think will float or sink before exploring items in the water tray.

Setting Up

- Fill the water tray with clear water. Alongside, arrange items that float (corks, sealed plastic bottles, pieces of wood, pumice stone, plastic toys and table tennis balls) and items that sink (stones, shells, marbles and balls of Plasticine).
- Add a selection of materials that will sink or float, for example cotton wool, bubble wrap, foil sheets and various types of fabric.

Do our boats sink or float?

Language and Literacy

- Talk about the children's experiences at bath-time. What toys do they play with? Do the toys sink or float?
- Add magnetic and sponge letters to the water tray. Do they sink or float? Add soap bubbles to the water so that the letters are hidden. Take turns to find a letter and identify it.
- Make a book about 'floating and sinking'. Draw round objects that float and objects that sink. Write clear labels alongside the drawings.
- Ask each child to write their name on a card and to put an object that floats and an object that sinks onto their card. Encourage them to take turns to talk to the other children about their chosen objects.
- Display boats made by the children (see Creative Work) against a blue background to represent water. Ask a child to talk about one of the boats on the display, explaining what the boat is made of and describing its colour and size. See if other children can guess which boat it is from the description.

Mathematics

- Look at the display of boats made by the children. Use appropriate language, for example to describe the 'biggest' and 'smallest' boats and to decide whether boats are 'above', 'below' or 'next to' each other.
- Count the boats on the display. How many boats will float? How many will sink?
- Introduce appropriate language during floating and sinking activities (see Our World), such as 'float', 'sink', 'full', 'empty', 'size', 'sphere', 'top', 'bottom', 'below', 'under', 'heavy', 'light' and 'solid'.
- Compare sizes and shapes as you work with Plasticine.
- Emphasise the mathematical language in the story of *Mr Archimedes' Bath* while dramatising the action with model people and animals. Talk about 'water level' and use the words 'rise' and 'fall', 'above' and 'below', 'more' and 'less'.
- Count how many stones or model animals need to be added to a jug half-full of water before it spills over the top.
- Sort objects that float and sink into two sets by putting them into separate containers on the table as they are taken out of the water.
- Introduce only spheres to the water, such as various balls, fruit and stones. Talk about the shape and whether the spheres float or sink.

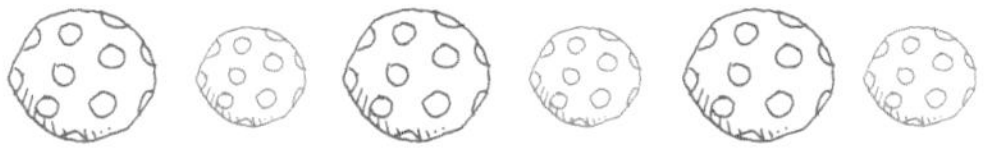

- Dramatise the story of *Mr Archimedes' Bath* using a blue sheet to represent the bath water. Ask each child in a group to be one of the animals. Sit the children in a line behind the sheet and tell them to stand up as their animal is mentioned and to pull the sheet up higher until, at the end of the story, all the children are standing behind it.

- Reread *Mr Archimedes' Bath.* Use a small transparent bowl or jug to represent the bath. Half-fill it with water and stick some tape to the outside at the level of the water. Add stones or heavy objects representing Mr Archimedes and the animals, one by one. What happens to the water level? Take the models out, one by one. Now what happens?

- Give each child a ball of Plasticine. What do they think will happen when they drop these into the water? Let them test their ideas. Ask the children to try to make a small dish shape with the Plasticine. Now what happens? Try different shapes.

- Ask each child to choose an empty plastic bottle and to check the top is screwed on tightly. Put the bottles in the tray. Is it possible to make them sink? Remove the bottles and take off the tops. Put the bottles in the tray and see what happens. Can the children make them sink? What do they need to do?

Our World

- Choose an object from the table to put into the water tray, and record whether the object floats or sinks by putting a cross into one of two columns on a piece of paper. Count the crosses in each column. Did more objects float or more sink?

- Take a stone and a table tennis ball and ask the children to guess which will float and which will sink. Drop them in the water tray to find out. Ask the children to take turns to choose an object from the table that they think will sink and another that they think will float. Why do some objects sink and others float?

- Talk about the children's experiences of learning to swim. What helps them to float? Look at armbands and pictures of buoyancy aids, such as life jackets and life buoys. Experiment with materials, such as bubble wrap, cork and string, to make miniature life jackets for model people.

- Cut out a jug-shaped piece of card, or a rectangle of card, to represent a cross-section of the water tray. Paint a blue line across it to represent the surface of the water. Lie the silhouette flat. After experimenting to see if objects float or sink, put each object on the card – along the surface line if it floats and below if it sinks. Draw and label the objects.

Creative Work

- Dip sponges into paint and splurge, drag or pat them across paper to create pictures. Display and add labels: 'We explored things which float.' 'We created these pictures with sponges.'

- Print patterns with items that float, such as corks and sponges. Print patterns with items that sink, such as stones. Compare the pictures and create a display with labels explaining how the pictures were made.

- Try rolling sealed plastic bottles across the surface of the water in the water tray. Roll the same bottles across a layer of paint and then over paper to create 'watery' patterns.

- Try to make boats that will float, from recycled materials.

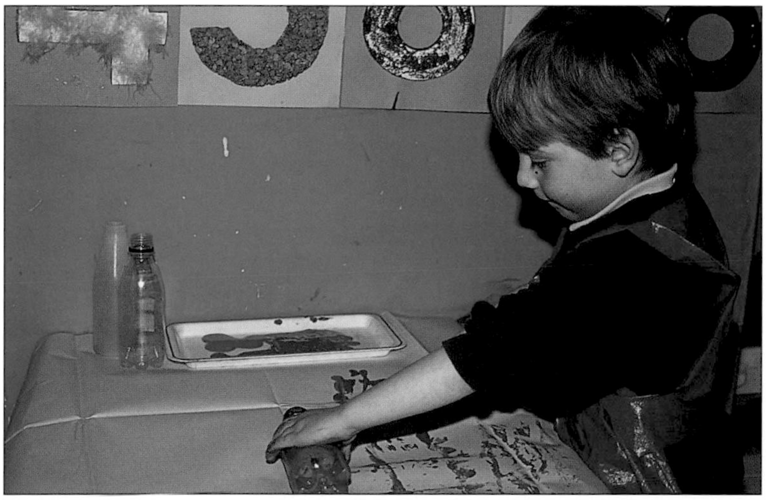

Home Links

Ask parents or carers to:

- point out how the water level rises when their children get into the bath, and how it falls when they get out

- help their children to complete a sheet recording whether everyday items at home float or sink

- try floating less familiar items in the bath, such as a pumice stone or a balloon.

Moving Across Water

Learning Intentions

- To question why things happen and how things work.
- To be able to select the tools and materials needed to create floating models.
- To extend vocabulary related to boats and ships and their purpose, and to make up stories using models.

Starting Point

- Look at books and pictures of different types of boat. Talk about how they are powered and the things they transport.

Setting Up

- Colour the water in the water tray with blue and green colouring to represent sea, river or lake water. Float model ships and boats in the water.
- In the water tray, create islands from small groups of stones. Add a model lighthouse made from a water-filled plastic bottle. Place an empty 'ball', used for clothing detergent, over the lid for the light.
- Create a jetty, using a wooden box or ice cream container with a lid, from which miniature model people can moor and launch boats. Weigh the box down by putting stones inside to stop it floating away.

Language and Literacy

- Look at books about water transport and introduce new words, such as 'ferry', 'houseboat', 'cruise liner', 'submarine', 'pirate ship', 'tanker' and 'rowing boat'. Compare the vessels.

- Make up stories using model people and the children's model boats in the water tray (see Creative Work). For example, invent imaginary journeys through storms or voyages to desert islands.

- Encourage the children to describe their experiences of travelling on the water. Ask: 'Have you ever been a ferry passenger?' 'Was the sea calm or rough?' 'Did you enjoy the journey?' 'Have you ever seen a lighthouse?' 'Can you remember where?'

- Create a houseboat from a square climbing frame for role-play. Surround the 'boat' with blue fabric to represent water. Ask the children what they will need to take onto their boat. Make up stories about life on board.

Mathematics

- Stand small model people and animals on stone islands in the water tray and ask questions such as: 'How can you cross from one island to another?' Make suitable bridges, boats or rafts from items such as stones, wooden rulers, string and plastic trays.

- Time how long it takes to move a model boat from one side of the water tray to the other using a paper fan. Repeat, using a straw to blow the boat along. Which was the quickest method?

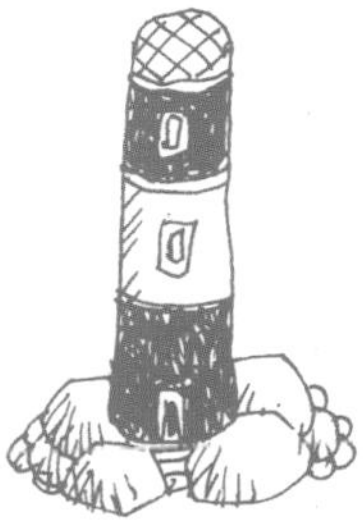

- Make a bridge from a strip of wood so that miniature model people can cross the water. Introduce the mathematical language associated with position, for example ask the children to put a figure 'on' the bridge and a boat 'under' the bridge. Use similar sentences to introduce 'above', 'below', 'beside', 'up' and 'over'.

Our World

- Try moving water with kitchen utensils and water play toys, such as whisks, jugs, water wheels, pumps and siphons. Is it possible to create waves? Put a model boat on the waves. What happens?

- Make a simple yacht with a foil tray. Thread a straw in and out of a sheet of paper for a sail and attach to the tray with Plasticine. Blow the yacht along using a small battery-operated fan. Try different-sized sails and compare the speed of the yacht.

- What happens to boats in storms? Look at pictures and models of lighthouses and discuss their purpose.

- What can be used to stop ships and boats moving? Look at pictures of anchors. How could the children anchor their own models? Experiment by tying different objects that float and sink, such as a cork or a stone, to the model with string. What happens when they try to blow the model along? Which of the objects stops a boat moving?

Creative Work

- Create a model boat that will sail in the water tray. Look in books for ideas and choose a type of boat or ship. Try a range of recycled materials, such as plastic trays, foil dishes and boxes. Put model figures in the boat and see if it still floats.

- Cover a table in blue material and display the children's model boats on top, along with other items such as miniature wooden boats in glass cases and model lighthouses. Include paintings of boats mounted on brightly coloured paper with name cards below. Paint a large life buoy as a frame for the central picture in the display.

- Create boats out of fabric and paper collage materials and display on a painted sea scene.

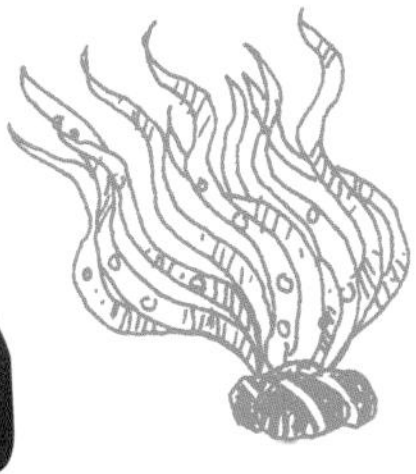

Home Link

Ask parents or carers to:

- encourage their children to play with toy boats at bath-time.

Colours

Learning Intentions

- To speak confidently in front of others, make personal choices and use initiative.
- To become aware of likes and dislikes.
- To respond in a variety of ways to stimulating experiences involving the senses of sight, smell and touch.

Starting Points

- Read stories involving colour, such as *Elmer* by David McKee and *The Mixed-up Chameleon* by Eric Carle.
- Change the colour and smell of the water in the water tray daily, by adding food colourings and essences.

⚠ **Note:** Check there are no children with allergies to food colourings, dyes, essences or soaps.

Setting Up

- Half-fill a transparent water tray with water. Alongside, cover a table with a towel and arrange four transparent plastic bowls and four jugs. Fill the jugs with water. On a tray, place a selection of food colourings, crêpe paper squares in bright colours and droppers.
- Create colours to add to the water in the tray. Take turns to colour water in a bowl or jug using droppers and food colouring. Wave crêpe paper backwards and forwards in the water to release its coloured dye. Choose one of the colours to add to the water tray.
- Try adding two different colours and seeing what happens.

Language and Literacy

- Teach the children the names of the colours used and introduce words such as 'darker', 'lighter', 'shade' and 'transparent'.
- Make a display of coloured circles and write the initial letter sound of each colour in the centre. Point to the colours one by one, emphasising the initial letter sound of each one as you say it.
- Ask individual children to explain to the rest of the group how they created the different colours in their bowls.
- Talk about the smells and textures they notice during the activities and encourage the children to express their likes and dislikes.
- Ask the children to explain to others how they made the pictures and flowers on their 'blue' wall display (see Creative Work).

Mathematics

- Ask the children to draw a picture on a small square of paper using their favourite colour crayon. Arrange these squares according to colour to create a block graph of favourite colours.
- Create a colour theme display beside the water tray. Display items of one colour, such as buckets, funnels, bricks and small model figures that are all red. Colour the water to match. Ask the children to find five different red objects or two red objects that are nearly the same.
- Use appropriate language to describe the quantities of colouring needed, such as 'a tiny drop', and introduce the terms 'full' and 'empty'. Compare the sizes of the water tray, bowls and jugs. Talk about how much liquid each holds.
- Place an empty cup beside each of the children's bowls of coloured water. Invite the rest of the children to choose their favourite colour of water, and to put a counter in the cup beside it. Count them to find the most popular colour.

Our World

- Drop diluted food colouring onto filter paper or paper towels using a dropper. Talk about what happens to the liquid when it lands. Drop two different colours next to each other. What happens when the colours meet? Mount the pictures in a display and entitle it, 'We have been exploring colours'.

- Add items to water to create different textures and talk about how they feel. Mix a thick slimy paste of cornflour and water and ask the children to try to lift it up with their fingers. What happens? Add cooked pasta shapes to make a tray full of 'snakes' or 'worms'. Can the children hold them with their hands?

- Mix soap flakes and water together to make stiff 'snow' and try to build a snowman. Talk about how the different mixtures feel. Which one do the children prefer?

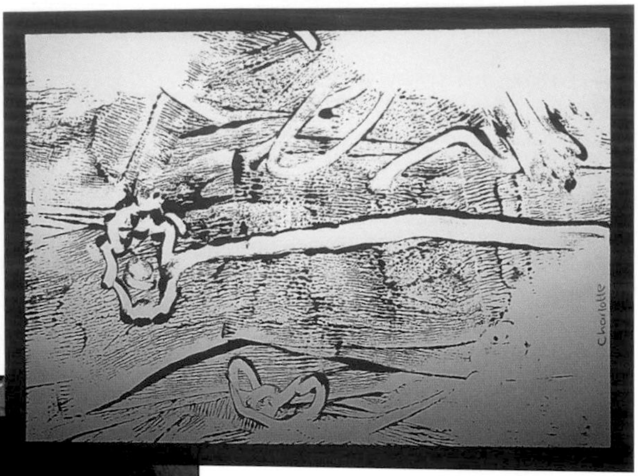

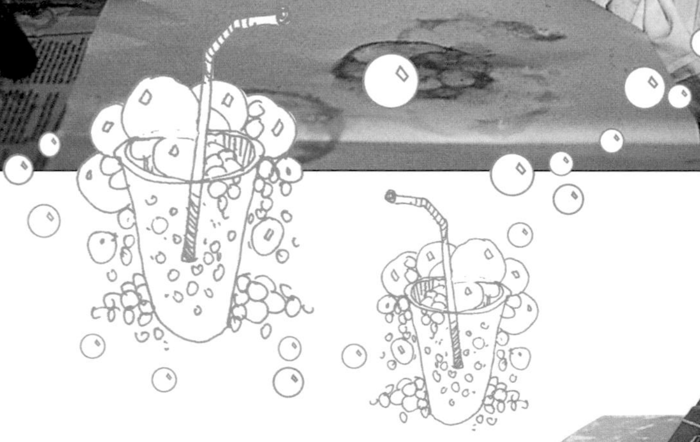

- Add different perfumes to the water, such as food essences, vinegar or liquid coffee. Talk about what the smells remind the children of. What are their favourite smells?

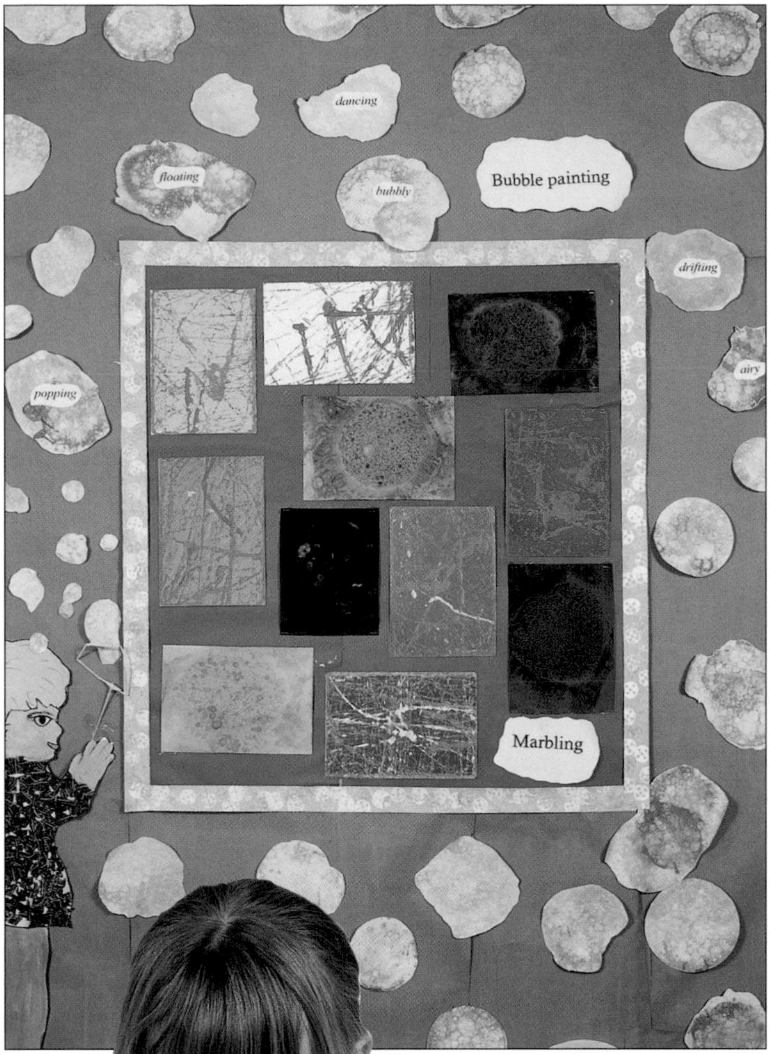

Creative Work

- Create symmetrical designs on paper by dropping different coloured blobs of paint onto one half and folding it over.
- Add washing-up liquid to coloured water in the water tray and blow bubbles through straws and tubes. Put pieces of paper on top of the bubbles to create patterns.
- Mix powder paint with cooking oil and drop this slowly onto water in a tray. Swish the paint gently around until it forms a marble pattern. Gently lower a sheet of paper onto the surface of the water and peel it back to reveal the pattern.
- Create a wall display of blue items. Include fabrics and children's blue painted pictures and collages. Cut out and mount pictures from magazines and calendars which have blue as the predominant colour. Display blue items brought in from home by the children on a table or shelf below the wall display.

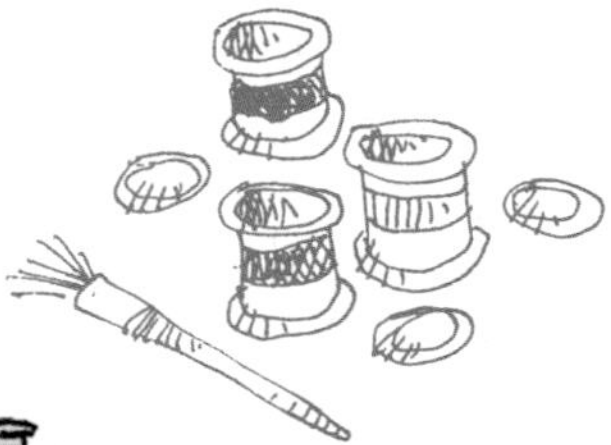

Home Links

Ask parents or carers to:

- make a drawing in their favourite colour to add to the block graph
- help their children create a cornflour and water mixture or simple marble pictures by following step-by-step instructions.

Vegetable Mixtures

Learning Intentions

- To discover features of vegetables and to explore the properties of some natural materials.
- To look closely at similarities, differences, patterns and changes.
- To handle a range of different tools and objects safely and with increasing control.

Starting Points

- In a group, explore and name the contents of a sack of vegetables.
- In the water tray area, set up a tray with tins and packets of vegetables for the children to examine.
- Using a selection of tools (scrubbing brushes, plastic pan scrubs, washing-up brushes), wash a selection of vegetables in a clean bowl of water in the water tray. Include some leaf vegetables, such as cabbage and celery.
- Visit a market stall or supermarket to buy vegetables for soup and to look at more unfamiliar vegetables.

Setting Up

- Display a large bowl of scrubbed and washed vegetables, including less familiar vegetables such as sweet potatoes or okra.

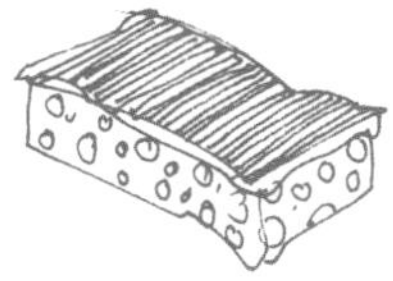

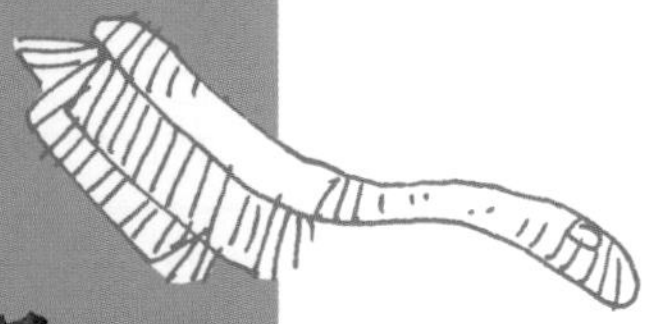

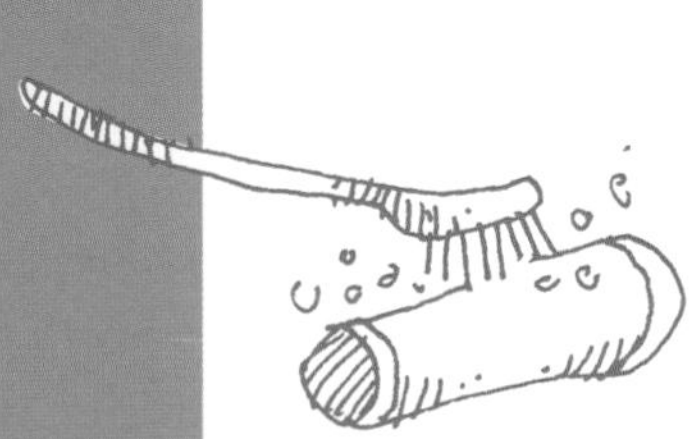

Language and Literacy

- Find some recipes for vegetable soup and talk about the ingredients. Help the children to illustrate and write out their own recipe card to hang on the notice board.
- Ask the children to think of words to describe the raw and cooked vegetables as they taste them in the Our World activities. Are they crunchy or soft, smooth or rough?
- Set up a role-play market stall for selling vegetables made of papier-mâché, plastic or salt dough. Help the children to write the names of the vegetables on labels.

Mathematics

- Provide plastic coins and a till for the role-play market stall. Decide on the amount to charge for each type of vegetable and help the children to write price tickets.
- Sort a pile of vegetables into sets of the same type.
- Arrange vegetables of the same type in order of size.
- Create patterns with vegetables, by arranging them in sequences or by printing with them.

Our World

- Observe vegetables closely through a magnifying glass and talk about how they feel and smell. Compare the shapes and colours. Look at books about vegetables and decide where each one grows. Point to the leaves, stem and roots.

- Help the children cut up a vegetable. Put the small pieces into a large pan and make some soup.

- Make comparisons between raw and cooked vegetables. Taste samples of both and discuss their taste and texture.

- Put dried peas in a tray with some water and observe any changes the following day. What has happened to the size, shape and texture of the peas?

- Explore the difference between mixing and dissolving. Make a jelly and talk about what happens to the jelly cubes when they are stirred in the hot water. Now add cubes of a vegetable to some hot water and stir. Does the same thing happen? Try mixing sand, wood shavings and dried clay with water. Make a simple chart of the substances that dissolve in water and those that do not.

Creative Work

- Print some pictures with the raw vegetables. Make unusual prints using half a cabbage and a celery leaf.
- Use collage materials to make a frieze showing the ingredients and utensils needed to make a pan of soup.
- Put chopped vegetables into a water tray full of clean water and make 'soup' using small pans and kitchen utensils. Role-play serving the soup in bowls.
- Take the water tray outside and use soil to make mud pies. Decorate with small stones and twigs. Leave the pies to dry in the sun.
- Cut out pictures of vegetables from magazines. Use these to make collage pictures. Display them in groups according to their predominant colour.

Home Links

Ask parents or carers to:

- make vegetable soup with their children at home, following a recipe written by the children
- encourage their children to help prepare the vegetables for a meal
- take their children to a supermarket and weigh some vegetables.

Daily Routines

Learning Intentions

- To understand the need for daily routines to maintain a healthy body.
- To show sensitivity and concern towards others.
- To develop an awareness of the passing of time by exploring everyday routines.

I wash my hands
This is the way we
wash our hands!

Starting Points

- Look at leaflets and posters on healthy eating and dental hygiene.
- Invite the community dentist to come to talk to the children about dental hygiene and healthy foods.
- Invite the community nurse or health visitor to come to talk to the children about hair care.

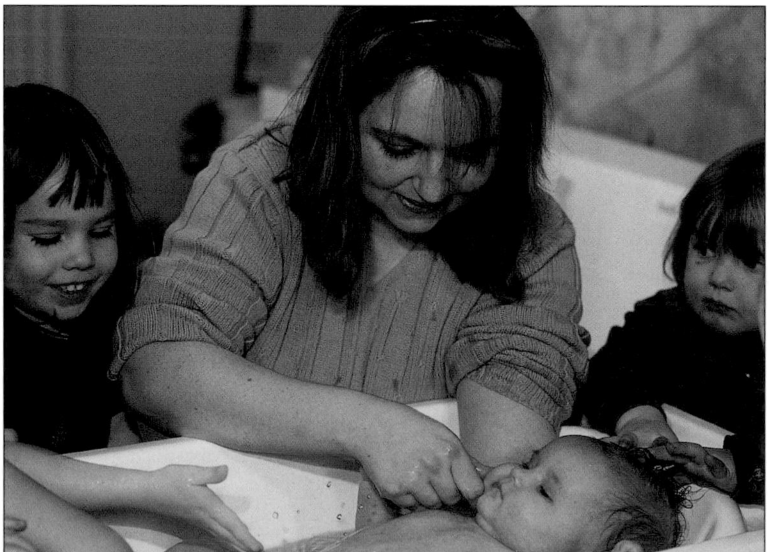

- Read books, poems and stories about daily routines such as *Bathtime* by Maureen Roffey.
- Talk about cultural differences in daily routines.
- Invite a parent to bring in a baby so the children can watch a bathing session. Let the children gently help with washing.

Language and Literacy

- Play 'I Spy' by saying, for example, 'I spy on my little table something beginning with ...' to introduce the initial letter sounds of items in the home.

- Role-play daily routines in the home corner with toothbrushes, mugs, a safety mirror, sponge, soap, face cloth, hairbrush and towel. Encourage the children to talk about the items they are using.

- Make a book about hygiene routines using photographs of the children, catalogue pictures, drawings and captions.

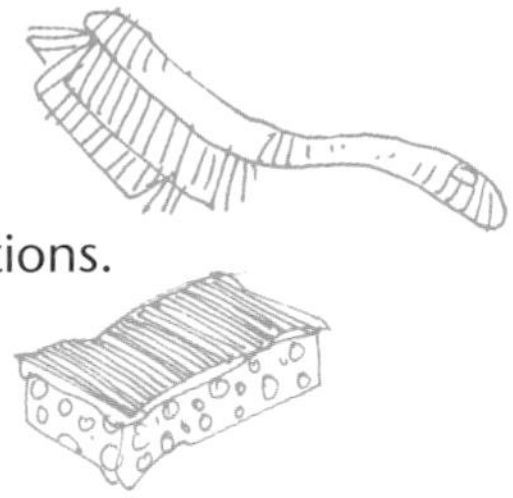

Mathematics

- Make a routines chart using card clock-faces with black pointers attached with split pins. Set each clock to represent the time a class routine starts, such as washing before snack-time or tidying up.

- Put three hoops on the floor and give each a different label, as follows: 'I can clean my teeth', 'I can get washed' and 'I can look after my hair'. Pass round a 'feely bag' containing items associated with each activity and ask individual children to take something out and put it in the correct hoop.

- Cut out pictures associated with cleaning teeth, washing and hair care from catalogues and leaflets. Sort into three subject piles and glue each set onto a circular piece of card. Label and hang as mobiles.

- Cover three yoghurt pots with red, yellow and blue paper. Make some toothbrushes using lollipop sticks with red, yellow and blue card 'bristles' glued to one end. Sort the brushes into the pots according to their colour.

Setting Up

- Set up a table display about routines associated with water such as cleaning teeth and washing. Include items such as a towel, a small bowl, a sponge, empty bubble bath and shampoo containers, a toothpaste box, a new toothbrush, a flannel and soap. Sit two clothed dolls beside it.

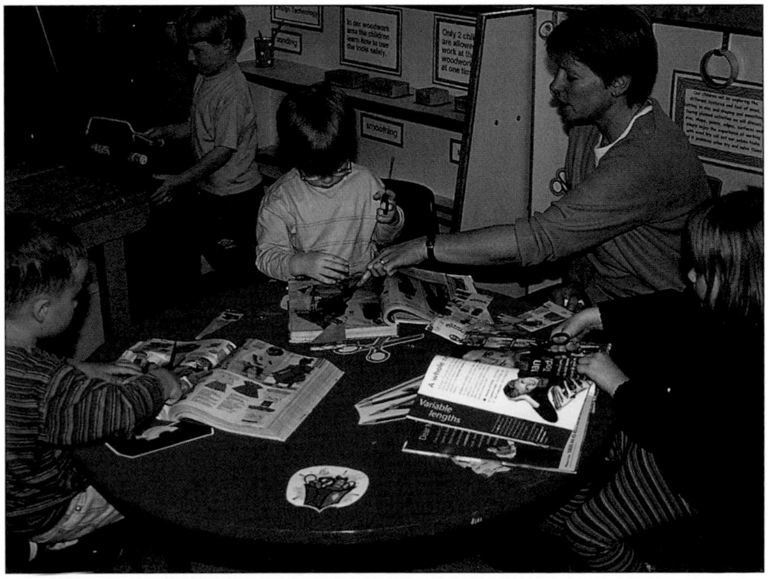

Our World

- Undress dolls and bathe them in tepid water in a baby bath. Use items from the washing display such as sponges and towels. Talk about the need to handle babies gently and to ensure that they are kept warm but not too hot.

- Dirty a doll with smears of washable paint without the children seeing. Encourage the children to try to clean the dolls in water without using soap. Ask them what is missing. Wash the dolls again with soap and talk about whether it removes the dirt more efficiently. Test different types of soap and bubble bath.

- Supply squares of material, such as towelling, shiny cotton, carrier bag plastic, woollen fabric, kitchen roll and foil. Ask the children which of the squares they think will dry the dolls best. Let them test their ideas. Introduce the word 'absorbent' by talking about how the fabric 'soaks up' the water.

- Record the results of the above activity, showing fabrics that would make good towels and those that would not.

⚠ **Note:** Always use non-toxic, non-allergenic detergents.

Creative Work

- Explore the smell of different bubble baths and soaps. Which do the children prefer?
- Ask the children to draw and paint pictures of toothbrushes and hairbrushes for your display.
- Use sponges, face-cloths and nail brushes to make patterns with paint for display.
- Create a bathroom scene by painting a picture of a washbasin with a child standing beside it. Create foil taps and plastic soap and add a small towel and sponge.
- Make some simple collage pictures of baths using a bath-shaped outline and squares of tissue paper. Mount the finished pictures on contrasting coloured paper.
- Create a wall display of the children's paintings and collage work. Make two large silver tap shapes and attach to the top of the display. Hang long strands of blue Cellophane from the taps to represent running water.

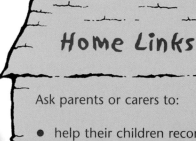

Home Links

Ask parents or carers to:

- help their children record the times of their daily routines
- let their children bring in personal items used in routines at home, such as their hairbrush or favourite bubble bath.

Washing Clothes

Learning Intentions

- To increase vocabulary associated with washing and clothes.
- To use language to make up stories, recreate roles and discuss experiences.
- To begin to develop an awareness of the difference between past and present events.

Starting Points

- Read *Mrs Lather's Laundry* from the 'Happy Families' series by Allan Ahlberg. Talk about the old-fashioned things Mrs Lather uses to wash the clothes. How are the children's clothes washed nowadays?
- Handle old-fashioned washing artefacts such as washboards, and look at recent catalogues of washing machines.
- Visit a museum to see an old-fashioned laundry and then visit a launderette.

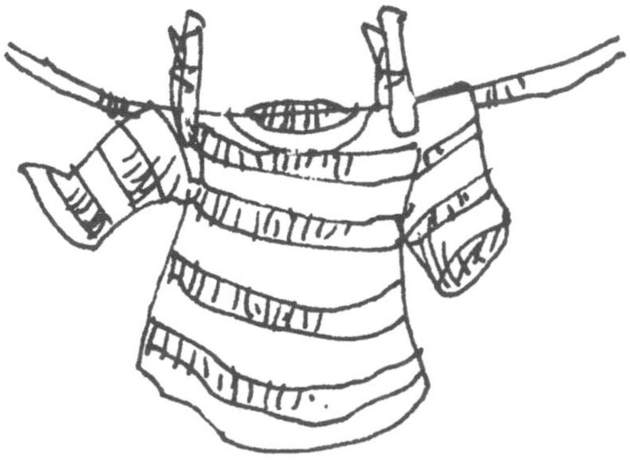

Setting Up

- Create a 'Washday – Past and Present' corner in the waterplay area. Include items such as a washboard, posser, scrubbing brushes, wooden tongs, bars of soap, towels, dolls' clothes to wash, and buckets or bowls to rinse the clothes. Also include a washing line and clothes horse.
- Place two washing baskets for wet and dry clothes and a child-sized mop, ready for any spills nearby.
- Add a toy washing machine, or one made from cardboard boxes.
- Prepare a stimulus display table with items brought in by the children, such as empty washing powder and fabric conditioner containers, wooden and plastic pegs, and washing machine and tumble dryer catalogues.

Language and Literacy

- Reread *Mrs Lather's Laundry* and make a list of the clothing she washed. Discuss the meaning of 'laundry' and 'customers' and name the old-fashioned items used such as the 'washboard', 'scrubbing brush', 'mangle', 'flat iron' and 'boiler'.
- Look at the clothes on the washday display and think of different words to describe their size, colour and what they feel like.
- Make a 'washday' book. Include drawings of modern washing machines and observational drawings of old-fashioned washday artefacts.
- Draw a washing line and stick on clothes cut from catalogues. Label the pictures.
- Sing the rhyme 'Mother's Washing, Mother's Washing' from *This Little Puffin*, edited by Elizabeth Matterson, and mime the actions.
- Set up a washing line. Encourage the children to role-play Mrs Lather using old-fashioned artefacts and several washing baskets. Use dolls for the babies Mrs Lather washed.
- Cut out card letters and hang them on a washing line. Ask the children to choose a letter each day, and to find things which begin with that letter.

Mathematics

- Count the pegs or clothes hanging on a line.
- Sort dolls' clothes into clean and dirty piles, or dry and wet washing into two wash baskets.
- Group the clothes pegs into different colours, materials or types.
- Match pairs of socks according to their size, colour, pattern or design.
- Compare the weight of wet and dry clothes using appropriate language, such as 'heavy', 'heavier' 'heaviest'; 'light', 'lighter', 'lightest'.

Our World

- Discuss the items brought in by the children for the stimulus table display and decide what they are used for.
- Talk about how washing machines, tumble dryers and irons work. Make a list of things in the kitchen that are powered by electricity. Emphasise the dangers of electricity.
- Invite grandparents to come to talk to the children about their memories of washdays in the past.
- Role-play all the washday tasks (washing, wringing out, drying and ironing) in the 'washday corner'.
- Wash dolls' clothes in warm water in the water tray using the washboard, scrubbing brushes and soap. Rinse the clothes in a bucket or bowl and hang them on the clothes horse and a washing line.
- Make comparisons between washing clothes in cold and warm water, with and without soap, and with a bar of soap, liquid soap or soap powder.

⚠ **Note:** Check for allergies first.

- Wash two similar items that dry relatively quickly, such as handkerchiefs. Let the children feel them both and then hang one indoors and one outdoors. Check both every half hour to see which dries first. Is it windy, sunny or damp outside?

Creative Work

- Use clothes pegs and card to make butterflies. Fold a piece of card in half and cut out the shape of a butterfly's wing. Open up the card and decorate it with felt-tipped pens or paint. Glue the peg down the centre to represent the body.

- Hang the butterflies to make a mobile or attach to a flower made from wire and tissue paper.

- Make dolls using a peg for the body, pipe-cleaners for the arms and collage scraps for clothes. Attach string to two pencils standing upright in clay, to make a washing line and use paper-clips to hang tiny clothes made from scraps of fabric.

- Screw up a small piece of towelling and clip a peg to it. Holding the peg, dip the towelling in paint and explore the effects of dragging and dabbing on paper.

- Make patterns using a rope washing line. Dip the rope into thick paint and lay it down as a curly line across one half of a large sheet of paper. Leave one end of the rope sticking out over the edge. Fold the paper over the rope and hold it down while pulling out the rope. Open the paper to reveal a pattern.

Home Links

Ask parents or carers to:

- encourage their children to count and match items of clothing at home

- help their children to make peg dolls and butterflies (give the children instructions to take home)

- contribute old-fashioned artefacts for display.

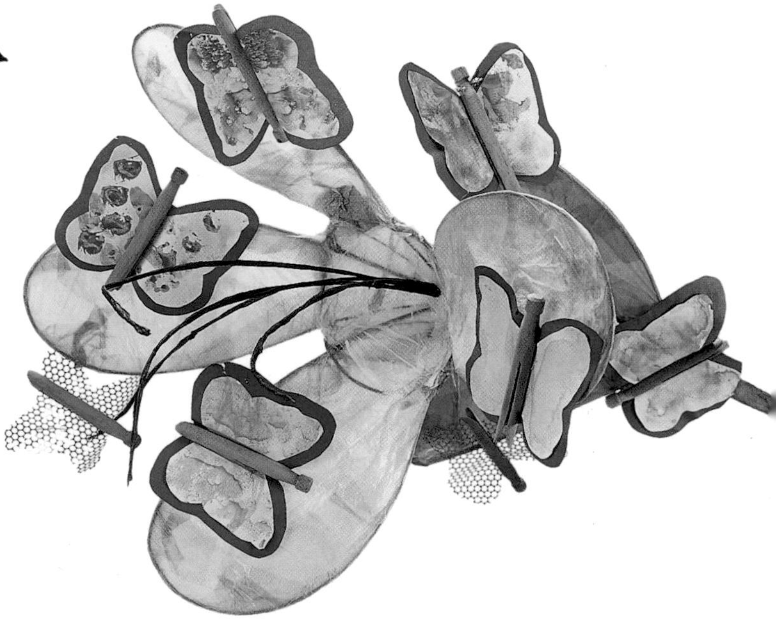

I'm a Little Teapot

Learning Intentions

- To respond to a rhyme and to imagine and recreate roles and experiences related to it.
- To become familiar with mathematical vocabulary and to solve simple problems associated with capacity.

Starting Points

- Sing the rhyme 'I'm a little teapot' from *This Little Puffin,* edited by Elizabeth Matterson, using appropriate actions.
- Look at the methods of making a cup of tea and the items used. Include both the quick method of putting a tea bag in a cup and the traditional method using tea leaves, a tea pot and a tea strainer.

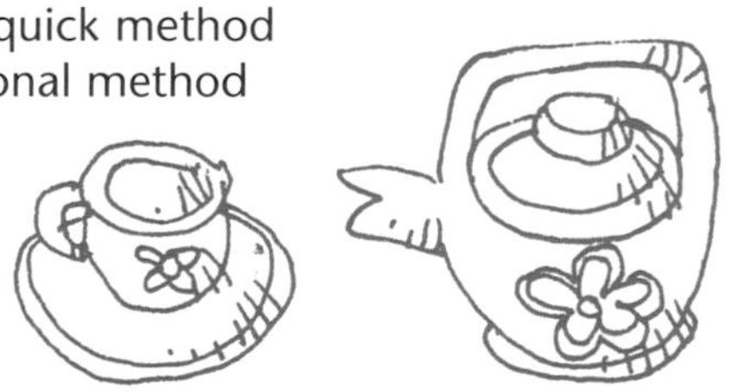

Setting Up

- Half-fill the water tray with water. Place a table nearby on which you can display plastic cups, saucers, a teapot, a sugar bowl and a jug. Stand different-sized metal teapots and some teaspoons alongside. Sit dolls down so that they can be served with tea.

Language and Literacy

- Sit some dolls in a circle and hold a tea party for them with cups of tea. Make up a story giving the reason for the party.
- Sing the rhyme 'I'm a little teapot'. Can the children point to the 'handle' and 'spout' on a teapot? Which other utensils have a spout or a handle? Introduce the word 'strainer' and associated words such as 'squeeze', 'drain', 'pour' and 'trickle'.

Mathematics

- Encourage the children to count the dolls. Ask them to collect the correct number of cups and saucers for the dolls so they can make them tea.
- Ask the children to measure one teaspoon of tea into the teapot for each doll. How many teaspoons will be needed?
- Match the cups to the saucers according to colour.
- Sing the rhyme 'I'm a little teapot' and talk about what is meant by 'short and stout'.
- Collect a range of different tea bags, including round, square, triangular and pyramid-shaped. Can the children name the shapes?
- Pour cold tea in the water tray to colour the water. Fill a teapot with cold tea and discover how many cups of tea can be made from a full teapot. Use phrases such as 'nearly full' and 'half empty', and make comparisons of size, such as 'bigger than', 'smaller than' and 'biggest'.
- Try to fill large lemonade bottles and fruit juice cartons with smaller containers using funnels.
- Pierce holes in plastic bottles at different heights. Fill the bottles with tea-coloured water and talk about what happens to the tea as it escapes. What do the children observe?
- Try filling unusual containers, such as a rubber glove or a hot water bottle, with water. Explore how the shape of the glove changes.

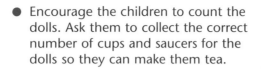

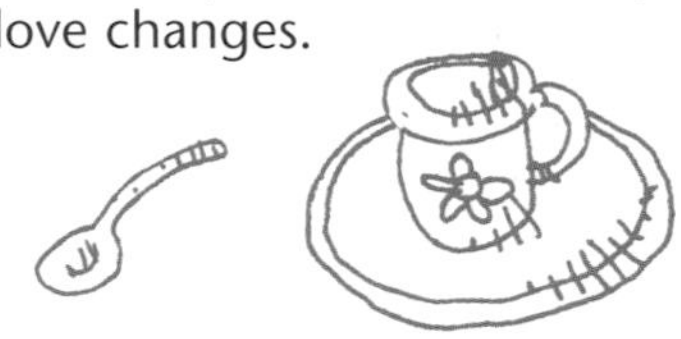

Our World

- Work with four children at the water tray. Give them a tea bag each and ask them to talk about what it looks like and how it feels. What do they think is inside the bag? How do they think the bag will make a cup of tea?

- Ask each child to fill a cup with water using a jug. Put a tea bag in the cup and stir. Very little colouring will come out. Tip the water out of the cups but leave the tea bags in them. Add hand-hot water and stir.

  ⚠ **Note:** Check the temperature of hot water before letting the children handle it.

- What else is sometimes added to a cup when making tea? Do the children drink tea at home? Do they like it with milk or sugar?

- Handle and smell loose tea leaves. Put a teaspoon of the tea leaves into the teapot, add hand-hot water to the pot and stir. What does the tea inside look like? What does it smell like?

- Pour loose leaf tea into a transparent plastic jug. Are there leaves floating about? Would the children like to drink the leaves? Show them a tea strainer and ask if they know what the holes are for. Let them take turns to hold the strainer while you pour the tea through it.

- Why do the children think some tea bags have a string and cardboard tag attached? Demonstrate how the tea bag can be stirred around and then lifted out before the tea is drunk. Does the string make it easier? How?

- Put damp tea leaves on a polystyrene tile. Use the tea as compost for growing mustard and cress seeds. Try different 'composts' such as soil, sawdust and cotton wool. Which is the most successful?

Creative Work

- Decorate biscuits and cakes with icing and small sweets for a grandparents, 'tea morning'.

- Create a role-play 'tea room' where children can serve staff, children or dolls with tea and cakes. Write and illustrate menus and posters. Make salt-dough cakes and biscuits. Decide on a name for the tea room and paint a shop-front name display.

- Use tea bags in collage work.

- Play a 'guess the drink' game. Put tea bags, coffee, chocolate powder and fruit shake powders in containers covered with netting. Ask the children to smell each container and guess what the drink is.

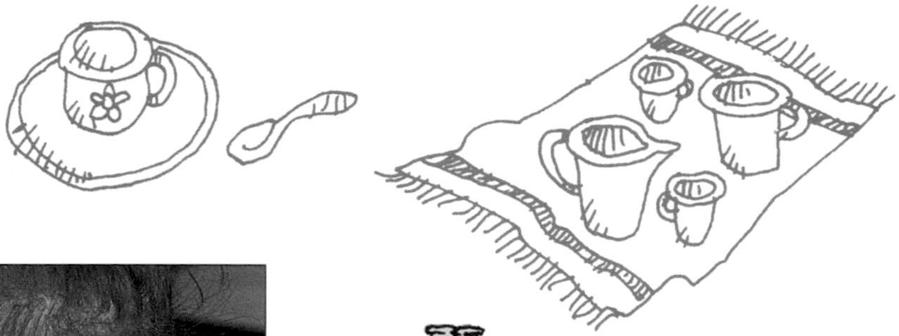

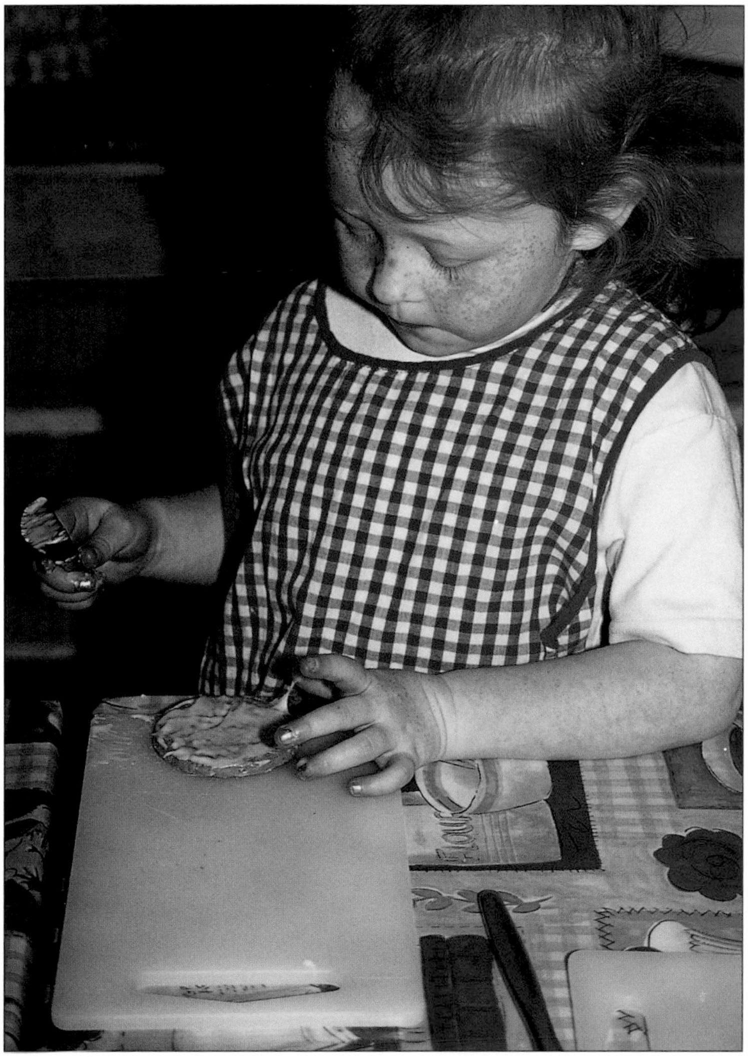

Home Links

- Invite grandparents to a 'tea morning'. Make some biscuits with the children beforehand and help them to arrange these carefully for their guests.

Ask parents or carers to:

- help their children learn the words of 'I'm a little teapot'

- take their children to a traditional tea room or café and talk about the range of drinks on the menu

- show their children the different types of tea for sale in a supermarket.

Rain

Learning Intentions

- To introduce vocabulary associated with position and size.
- To explore the properties of water, waterproof materials and absorbent materials.
- To encourage children to question why things happen.

Starting Points

- Learn rhymes about rain, such as 'I hear thunder', 'Dr Foster' and 'Incy Wincy Spider'. Make up actions to go with the words.

- Look through the window on rainy days to watch how the rain splashes into gutters, runs down windows and forms puddles on the ground. Discuss where rain comes from.

Setting Up

- Leave the water tray empty. Arrange the following items nearby: small and large watering cans, colander, sieve, shower nozzle, hosepipe and jug.
- Create a stimulus table display near the water tray with rainy-day items, such as an umbrella, rain hat and Wellingtons.

Language and Literacy

- Go outside dressed for a rainy day and carry umbrellas. If it is not raining, use a watering can to pour water over the children. Talk about how the rain feels. What can they hear? What do the children like or dislike about rain?

- Sing 'Rain, rain, go away, come again another day'. Emphasise the rhyming words, 'away' and 'day'.

- Use sieves, watering cans and colanders to make rain. Think of words to describe the sound of the rain, such as 'splish', 'splosh' and 'drip'. Write each word on a raindrop-shaped card to hang as a mobile.

- Supply rainy-day items and encourage the children to dress up in rainy-day clothes for role-play.

Mathematics

- Read the rhyme 'Dr Foster'. Talk about the puddle he stepped in. How deep would it have been to reach his middle?

- Stand a small model figure on a ball of Plasticine in a washing-up bowl to represent Dr Foster. Pour water on to 'Dr Foster' until the water comes 'up to his middle' using a watering can. Use the words 'deep' and 'shallow', 'middle' and 'tall'.

- Make Wellington boot prints. Look closely at the patterns. Are any of the soles the same?

Our World

- Try to make puddles indoors by covering the bottom of an empty water tray with a layer of sand and pressing it down to form depressions. What happens to water as the children pour it into the holes?
- Talk about waterproof and absorbent materials. Try covering the sand in the water tray with a refuse sack and a towel before pouring water on top. Which of the materials is absorbent and which allows puddles to form?

- Look at some puddles outdoors. Look at where they form and decide whether the surface of the ground is waterproof or absorbent.
- Try making a rain effect by piercing holes in plastic bottles, balloons, rubber gloves and yoghurt pots and pouring water through them.

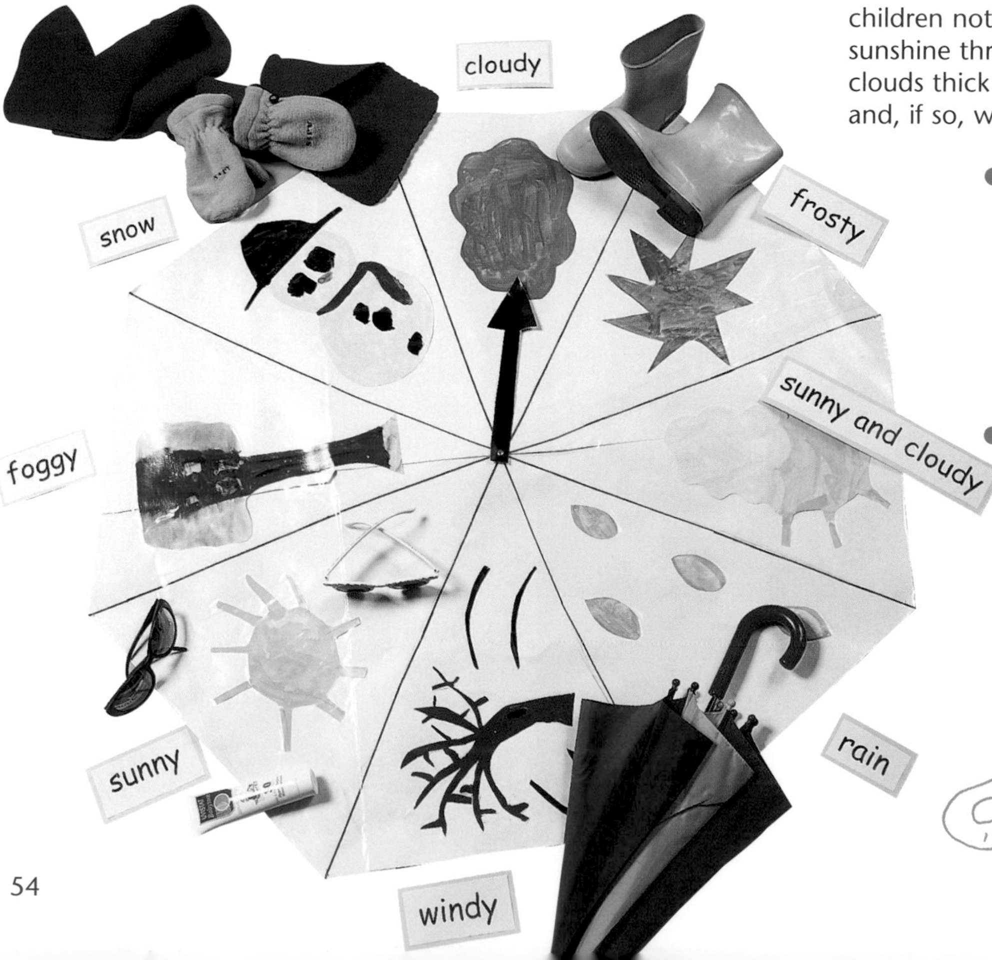

- Observe the clouds. What do the children notice? Can they see sunshine through the clouds? Are the clouds thick or thin? Are they moving and, if so, why?
- Talk about thunder and lightning. Have any of the children heard thunder or seen lightning? Discuss how they feel during a thunderstorm.
- Keep a daily weather chart and measure the rainfall in a simple rain gauge made from a cut-down plastic lemonade bottle with a funnel in the top.

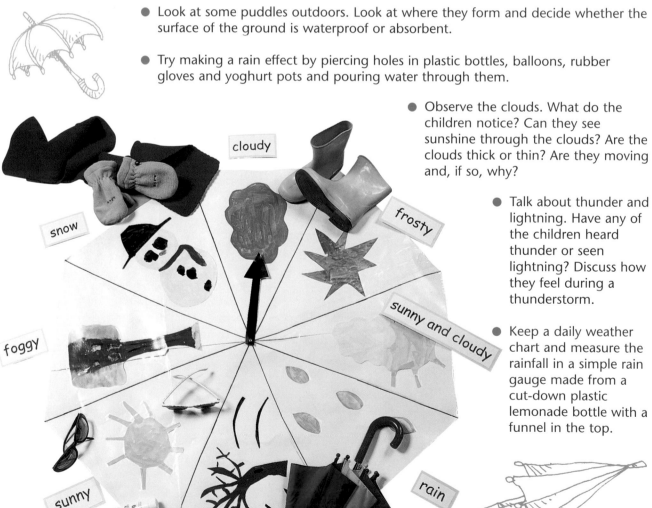

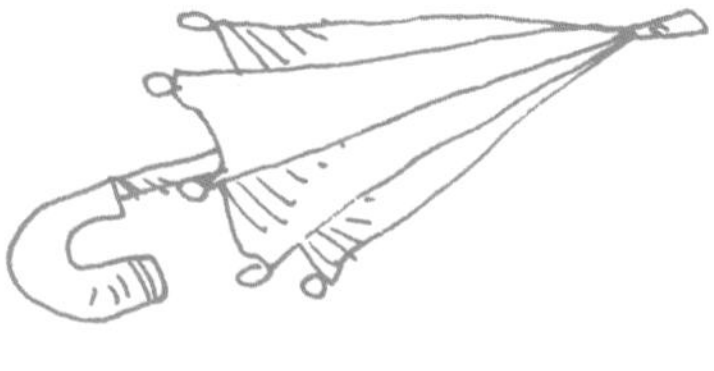

Creative Work

- Create a frieze entitled 'A rainy day' depicting one or two children with umbrellas in the rain. Use a range of collage materials and label appropriately.
- Create rain from watery paint and splash it onto paper to produce rain pictures.
- Watch rain run down the window and create the same effect on paper by blowing watery paint with a straw or holding the paper at an angle so that paint runs down it.

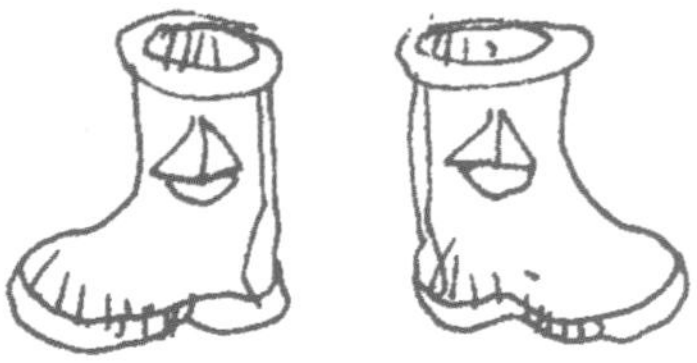

Home Links

Ask parents or carers to:

- take their children out on a rainy-day walk, wearing the appropriate waterproof clothing; pretend to splash through puddles and shelter under umbrellas
- look through a window on a rainy day with their children and talk about how the raindrops trickle down the window to form tiny rivers
- help their children to learn rainy-day rhymes and share them at home.

- Make a wall display with your rainy pictures and prints and add appropriate captions explaining how they were created.
- Explore sound by using percussion instruments to create the crashing sound of thunder and the pitter-patter of raindrops. Talk about the noise of raindrops on an umbrella or a roof. Drum fingers on a hard surface to create the sound of heavy rain falling on a roof.
- On the floor, place a long sheet of old wallpaper upside down on newspaper. Pour thick paint into a large shallow tray and ask the children to put their feet into the tray while wearing Wellington boots. Let the children walk along the wallpaper from one side to the other. Hold their hands so that they do not slip.

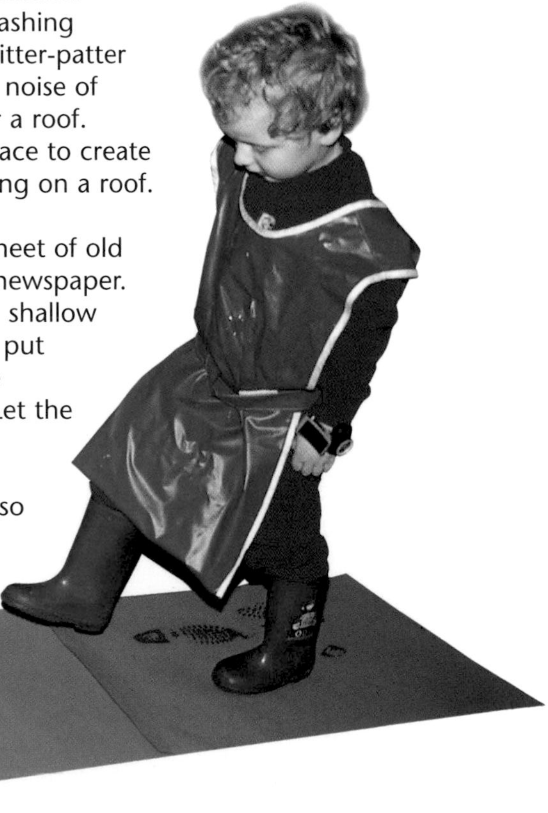

Mrs Plug the Plumber

Learning Intentions

- To enjoy and respond to stories and to explore the meanings and sounds of new words.
- To hear and say initial sounds in words.
- To use mathematical ideas and methods to solve practical problems and to use the appropriate language.

Starting Points

- Read the story *Mrs Plug the Plumber* by Allan Ahlberg.
- Visit a hardware store to look at the range of plumbers' pipes and to buy a selection of pipes and connections.
- Invite a plumber to come to talk to the children and to show some of the tools and materials they use.

Setting Up

- Half-fill the water tray. Arrange a selection of pieces of rigid and flexible plastic pipe of different lengths and thickness alongside, together with plastic connecting pieces and pouring utensils, such as jugs and cups.

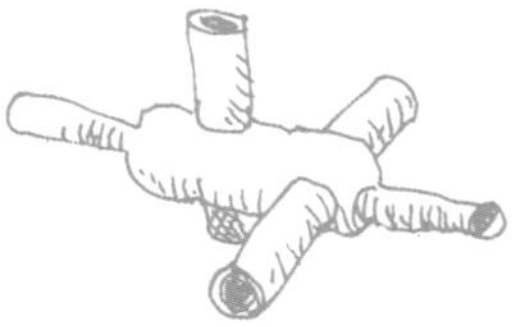

Language and Literacy

- Think of words that describe the noise and movement of water in pipes, such as 'gurgle', 'bubble' and 'trickle'.
- Introduce new words associated with plumbing, such as 'pipe', 'drain' and 'plumber'.
- Make a pipe-shaped book of things starting with the letter 'P'. Ask the children to draw pictures and cut them out of catalogues. Write labels under the pictures.
- Read *Mrs Plug the Plumber*. Talk about the contents of Mrs Plug's bag and discuss the meanings of new words, such as 'spanner', 'pliers', 'plunger' and 'blow lamp'. Fill a bag with the items and use as a prop when reading the story.

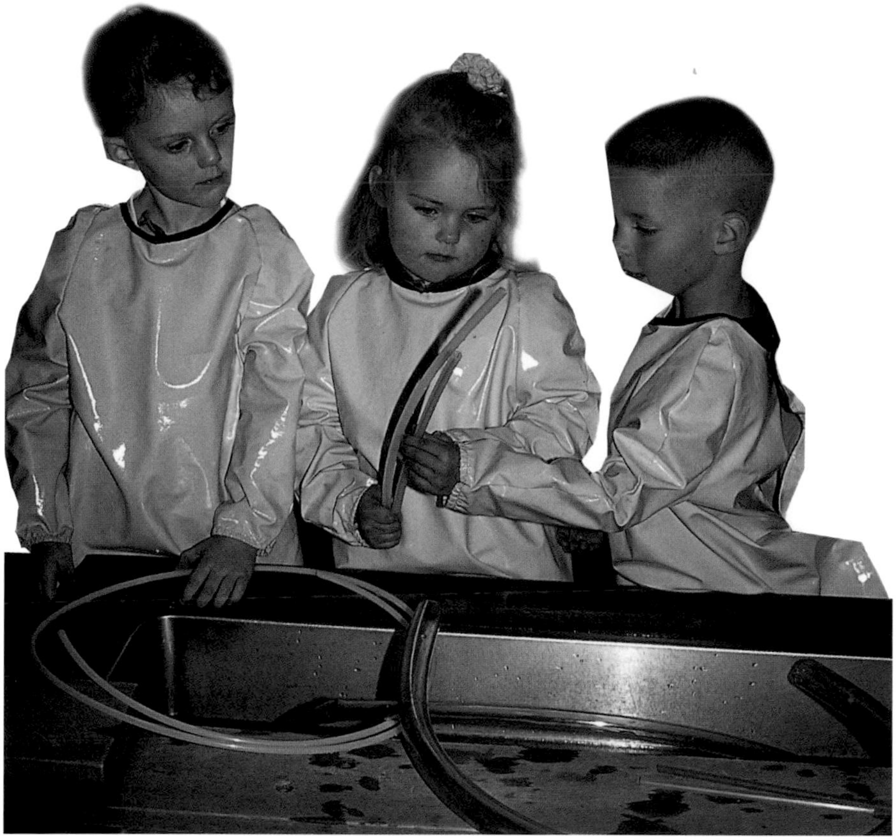

Mathematics

- Compare pieces of pipe using the appropriate mathematical language to describe width and length. Use opposite words, such as 'narrow and wide', 'thin and thick', 'straight and curved', 'long and short'.
- Put two hoops on the floor and sort the pipes into two sets, for example long and short, thick and thin. Count the pipes in each hoop.
- Sing 'Incy Wincy Spider', emphasising the meaning of the words 'up' and 'down' using pieces of the plastic piping and small plastic spiders on strings as you do so.
- Dangle a plastic spider on the end of a string down to the bottom of a pipe. Put the pipe into the water. Pull on the string to make the spider climb the pipe. Use jugs to pour water down the pipe. If the string is held loosely, the spider should be pushed back down by the 'rain'.
- Create repeat patterns by printing with pipes. For example, use pipes of two different diameters alternately.
- Make a miniature plumbing system in the water tray using pipes and plastic connections.

Our World

- Look for pipes on the outside of buildings, on a rainy day if possible. Point to drainpipes. What do the children think these are for? Talk about gutters and drains.
- Look for pipes on the inside of buildings. Look at the backs of sinks. Ask if the children know how water gets into taps and what happens when it goes down the drain.
- Lift the lid on a toilet cistern and watch as the toilet is flushed. Talk about how the clean water pours into the toilet to flush the dirty water down the drain.
- How do the pipe connection pieces work? Will all connectors fit all pieces of pipe? Why not? Why must the connectors fit tightly? What happens when pipes leak?
- Talk about how a plumber mends a leaking pipe. Make a hole in a flexible tube and try to seal it again using such things as a sticking plaster, insulating tape, a bandage and a strip of paper. Which of these items stop the water escaping? Introduce the word 'waterproof'.

- Read *An Evening at Alfie's* by Shirley Hughes to discover the effects of leaking pipes.
- Check that water flows freely through the plumbing system the children have constructed. Pour water through funnels into pipes and check for leaks.
- Seal the end of a pipe or use a plastic bottle for this activity. Pierce holes along the side. Stand it up and fill it with water. What do the children notice about how the water comes out of the holes? Is the force of the jet always the same?
- Can the children bend pieces of pipe? Introduce the word 'flexible'.

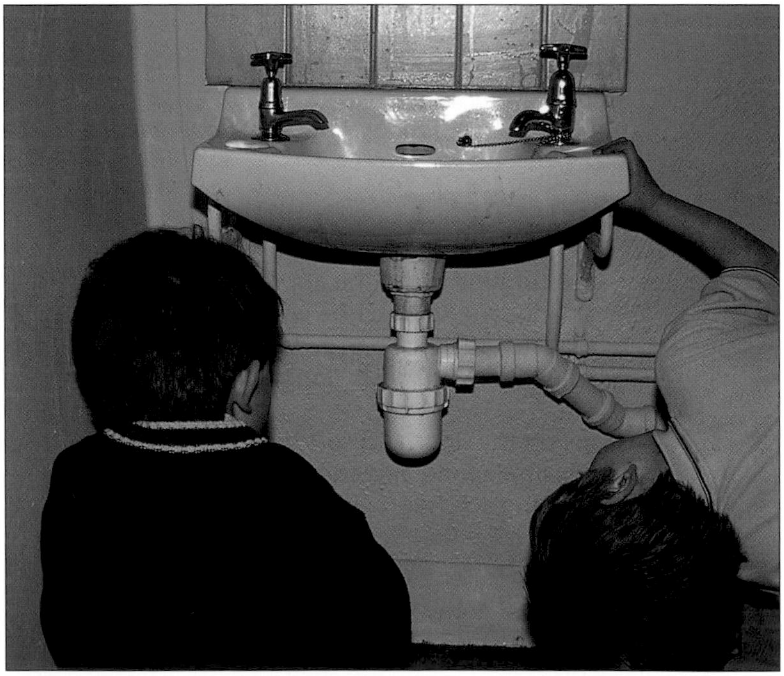

Creative Work

- Use the ends of pipes and connecting pieces to make prints. Discuss the different sizes of the prints made. Do they make the same shapes? Why?

- Roll lengths of pipe in paint and then onto paper to create patterns.

- Use small pieces of pipe to roll out dough. Then use the ends to make circular impressions and patterns.

- Use cardboard tubes, plastic bottles, gold and silver paint and foil to create 3D pipe structures. Arrange them to form a display. Try rolling marbles down the structures and predicting where they will emerge.

- Try making different noises by pouring water down the pipes in the water tray. Is there a difference in the sound if the pipe is thinner or thicker?

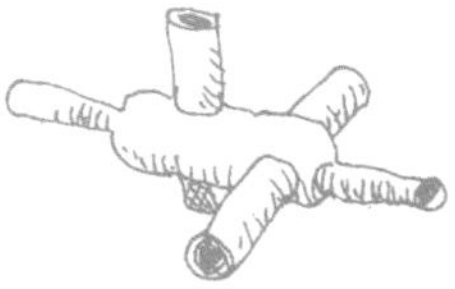

- Use pipes of different lengths to accompany songs and music. Try tapping the pipes together or using them as beaters against pans or tins.

- Suspend clusters of pipes of different lengths from strings to make wind chimes. Hang them near a window or on the branches of a tree.

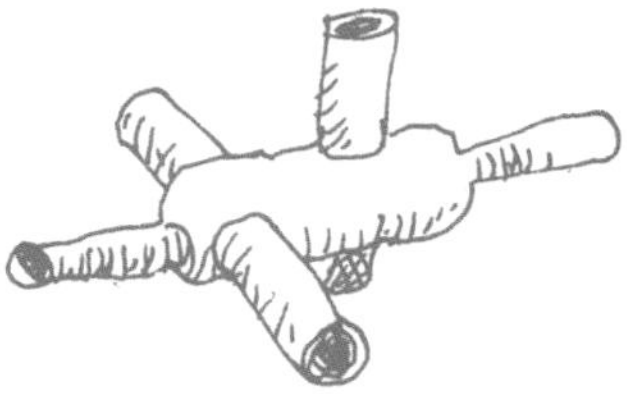

Home Links

Ask parents or carers to:

- show their children the plumbing and pipes at home and discuss how water arrives and leaves their home.

Noah and the Ark

Learning Intentions

- To discuss changes in the weather.
- To compare the features of living things.
- To sort, count and match animals, and put them into pairs.

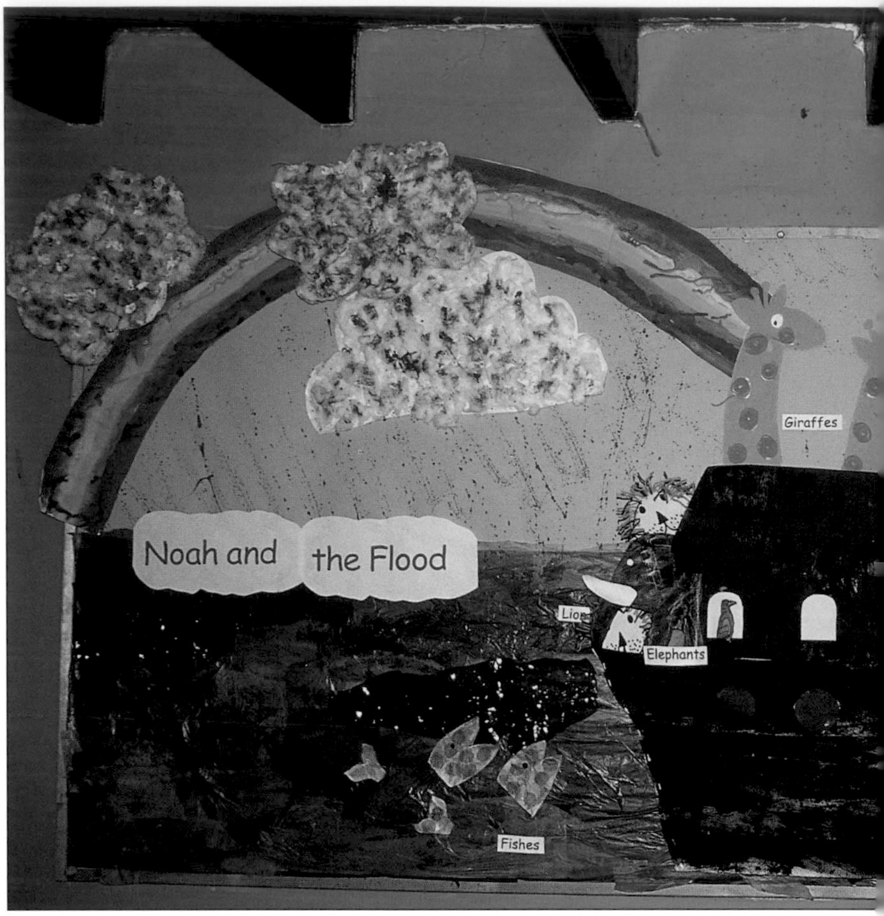

Starting Points

- Read the story of 'Noah's Ark' using props (model figures and animals and an ark made from a shoebox).
- Discuss different weather conditions. Have the children experienced a thunderstorm or seen a rainbow?

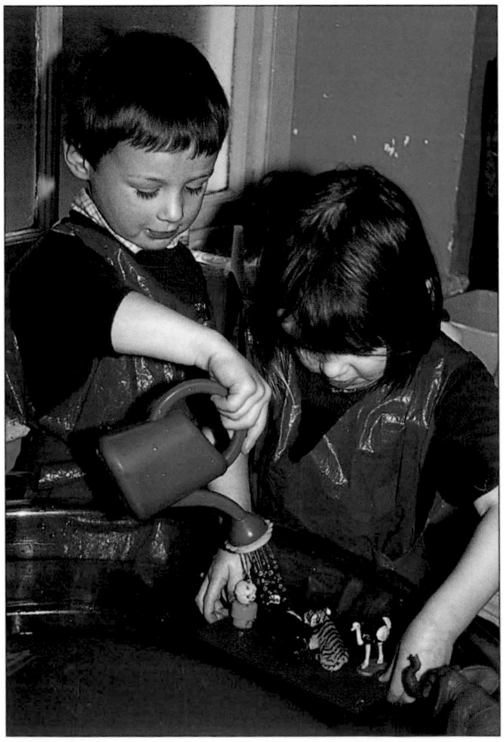

Setting Up

- Colour the water in the water tray blue. Nearby, arrange containers that can represent arks, such as plastic ice cream containers and tin baking trays. Add small model figures to represent Noah and his family, and model animals.

Language and Literacy

- Play a game in which each child picks up a named animal. Once they are familiar with the names, describe the animals and see if they can identify them.
- Write card labels for the animals and stand them in front of the models or add to a wall frieze.
- Create an ark from floor cushions and use soft toys to dramatise the story of Noah.
- Dramatise 'Noah's Ark'. Place a container to represent the ark in the water tray. Use a strip of wood as a plank and walk the animals down the plank to the ark. What will happen to the people and animals on the ark? Simulate rain using a watering can and make waves with a whisk or hands.

Mathematics

- Tip a box of model animals onto the centre of a table. Ask the children to take turns to pick a pair of animals to go into the ark.
- How many items make a pair? Name items that are usually in pairs. Match pairs of socks and gloves.
- Count the animals that will fit into an ark. Repeat with a different sized ark. Is the number the same?
- Make a graph of the different types of pet the children have. Which animal is the most popular? Which is the least popular?
- Make a game with pairs of matching cards showing pictures of animals. Turn the cards over and try to find two the same.

Our World

- Ask a child to choose an item from the table that they think will float. Try it in the water. Make a list of suitable materials for building an ark.

- Take it in turns to make rain over an ark using a watering can. How can the animals be kept dry? Construct a covered area in the ark.

- Have the children been on a boat? Have they been on a ferry? What can they remember about the journey?

- Talk about what the animals in the ark would need. What preparations would Noah make to see that the animals are well cared for? Do the children have pets? How do they care for them?

- Compare the features of the animals and birds going into the ark. Make and illustrate a book showing the textures and patterns of animal skins, or make a display that divides them into two groups, for example animals with four legs and birds with two legs.

Creative Work

- Create a 'Noah's Ark' wall frieze. Use blue paper for a backing, with rain clouds made from cotton wool glued along the top. Make the sea from strips of blue and green Cellophane, tissue and crêpe paper. Use corrugated paper for the ark shape and fabric scraps for the animals and people. For rain, spatter grey paint across the scene.

- Paint a large rainbow using watery paint so the edges of each colour merge. Attach to the wall above the water tray.

- Make stormy seas pictures. Create waves with finger painting and spatter blue paint across the paper with an old toothbrush.

- Talk about how animals move and then ask the children to move imaginatively to *Carnival of the Animals* by Saint-Saëns.

- Use musical instruments and the children's voices to accompany a dramatisation of 'Noah's Ark'. Include sounds to represent crashing thunder and waves, howling wind and heavy rain.

Home Links

Ask parents or carers to:

- come to watch your dramatisation of Noah's Ark

- take their children to a zoo and indentify males and females of the same species.

Useful Resources

There are many items that it is useful to have available when preparing to enjoy waterplay activities. The following lists are for guidance and inspiration only, and are by no means comprehensive. It is unnecessary to have every suggested item to participate successfully in waterplay projects. When choosing your resources, it is useful to look for sets in matching colours as these will add to the mathematical opportunities offered.

Specialised equipment

Most specialised equipment can be obtained from suppliers of children's educational materials. There are many options and price ranges to choose from.

- tabards (for the children)
- water tray and stand
- free-standing shelves for the stand base (to store equipment)
- waterwheels

Hardware

A variety of cheap, colourful utensils in different sizes can be found in hardware stores or department stores.

- paint roller trays
- flexible tubing
- plastic pipes and connectors

Kitchen equipment

Kitchen shops are a good source of brightly coloured plastic equipment. Try to obtain some items in as many different sizes as possible.

- funnels
- jugs
- sieves
- spoons
- potato mashers
- whisks
- slotted spoons
- spaghetti spoons
- measuring spoons

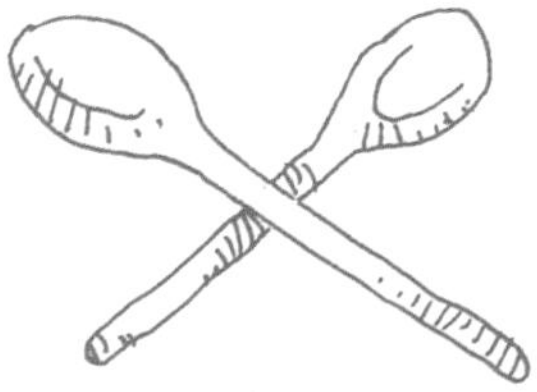

Recycled materials

Recycled packaging will provide an inexhaustible and environmentally friendly source of equipment. The items should be cleaned thoroughly and checked for sharp edges before use. It is useful to pierce some of the plastic containers at the base or at different levels with a hot knitting needle, so that they will sink and for experimental projects.

- plastic bottles (with and without screw tops)
- cartons
- yoghurt pots

Found objects

Make a collection of natural items. Be careful, however, to wash them thoroughly and check for sharp edges before use. Gather only discarded objects and remember not to remove items from protected landscapes.

- corks
- sponges
- shells
- stones
- pieces of wood

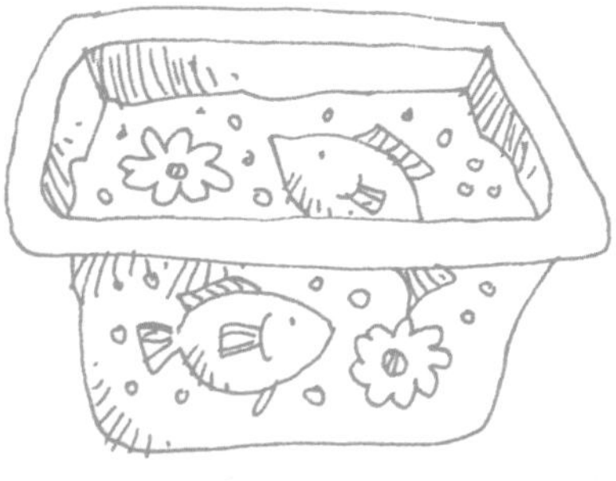